INSTRUCTOR'S MANUAL

7th edition
PRENTICE-HALL
HANDBOOK
FOR WRITERS

INSTRUCTOR'S MANUAL

MELINDA G. KRAMER

DONALD C. RIGG

7th edition

PRENTICE-HALL

HANDBOOK

FOR WRITERS

GLENN LEGGETT
Grinnell College

C. DAVID MEAD
Michigan State University

WILLIAM CHARVAT
Late of Ohio State University

Prentice-Hall, Inc., Englewood Cliffs, New Jersey 07632

10 9 8 7 6 5 4 3

ISBN: 0-13-695775-7

Printed in the United States of America

CONTENTS

INSTRUCTOR'S MANUAL

7th edition
PRENTICE-HALL
HANDBOOK
FOR WRITERS

INTRODUCTION

Writing skills, contrary to much popular student opinion, are part of the baggage individuals will need to carry with them into the future. "After I finish this course, I'll never have to write another paper" or "I don't need to know this grammar--my secretary will correct all my letters" are comments frequently heard in the halls outside English classes. Most students would rather be tied naked over an anthill than concentrate on the "dull, boring, useless, and picky" assignments in a text devoted to the fundamentals of grammar, rhetoric, and composition.

And yet, in later years, these are the same people who turn up in continuing education classes, business communications courses, and "executive brush-up" seminars--mumbling to each other "I wish I'd paid attention the first time." Despite all our telephones, copying machines, dictaphones, computers, and word processors, the ability to write a clear and communicative message is valued today more than ever before--perhaps because, like diamonds, the lucid sentence is an increasingly rare commodity.

The seventh edition of the *Prentice-Hall Handbook for Writers* is designed for people at both ends of the spectrum: those with on-the-job writing problems requiring a basic reference tool and those in structured classroom situations requiring a comprehensive text. This *Instructor's Manual*, however, is for *you*: the teacher confronting those students who habitually insist on making mountains out of their anthills.

The *Instructor's Manual* has two functions. First, it provides answers for the exercises in the seventh edition of the *Prentice-Hall Handbook*, saving your all-too-precious time for other class preparations. Second, it suggests guidelines and approaches that can be used with various sections of the *Handbook*. Experienced teachers may find reinforcement or new inspiration, and those teaching a writing course for the first time may appreciate the security of "something to fall back on."

The exercise answers and classroom suggestions in this *Manual* did not wash on shore in a bottle, nor were they pronounced by an oracle. They are simply offered in the spirit of helpfulness and are never intended in any way to supersede individual instructor judgment. Oftentimes, you may have alternative answers and ideas which are just as good, or perhaps even better than, those listed. Terrific. If you pass them along to us --who knows --they may even end up in the eighth edition. But our common goal remains: if we all pull together, in the end we can hope the students' need will have been served.

THE USES OF THE TEXT

First of all, the *Handbook* may be used exclusively as a reference tool. At the request of their instructors, students may study those sections of the text which refer to their specific writing problems. For example, while grading writing assignments, you may wish to note in the margin of a student's paper those portions of the *Handbook* he or she should consult for assistance in correcting errors. Similarly, students will be able to locate relevant text sections themselves as they read your comments.

A second way in which the *Handbook* may be used is as a combination reference tool and supplementary source for class work. Frequently, you will discover areas of weakness shared by the majority of a class. By reading text sections and doing the exercises as a class, students can benefit from concentrated exploration and instructor-led discussion of pervasive problems. Such a procedure also provides a basis for testing and additional writing assignments.

A third way in which the *Handbook* may be used is as the primary curriculum material for the course. When you wish to concentrate chiefly upon fundamentals or when students are particularly deficient in the basics of written language, the *Handbook's* explanatory sections and exercises can provide the backbone for an entire course in remedial English, basic grammar, or beginning composition. Combined with the *Prentice-Hall Workbook for Writers* and the *Prentice-Hall Diagnostic Test,* the *Handbook* becomes part of a complete writing-skills package designed for intensive work in grammar, punctuation, mechanics, spelling, and composition.

A fourth way in which the *Handbook* may be used is in addition to a rhetoric or reader in instances where you may want to emphasize training in fundamentals during the first part of a course. In such an instance, you can use the *Handbook* almost exclusively for awhile, then shift to the rhetoric or reader, continuing to use the *Handbook* as a supplementary text on an as-needed basis or for reference purposes.

THE ARRANGEMENT OF THE TEXT

The Prentice-Hall Handbook for Writers proceeds from the basic elements of written English to the larger elements of composition. After a brief introduction describing the growth of the English language, the text then discusses basic grammar. This section is followed by portions devoted to basic sentence faults, manuscript mechanics, and punctuation. Next, sections dealing with the larger elements of English composition focus on topic development, essay organization, the formulation of thesis statements, and paragraph writing. Following this, more sophisticated aspects of sentence structure, logic, and diction are investigated. Later sections of the text are devoted to the library and the research paper, writing summaries and examinations, letters, memorandums, and other business communications. The text concludes with an index to grammatical terms.

The above arrangement is obviously not the only way the material could have been presented. You may prefer to begin with the section on the whole composition, splicing in other sections as your class requires them. Or perhaps you feel more comfortable starting with the paragraph and building toward a complete composition. In some courses, on the other hand, basic grammar and sentence construction may be your primary focus. With these variations of approach in mind, the authors of the *Handbook* have structured the text so that the sections are more or less independent of each other.

Consequently, you can assign sections in any order that fits your classroom needs without problems of continuity. For example, the section on the research paper is placed toward the end of the text because research paper writing is assigned during the second term in many composition courses. If, however, you wish to introduce documentation earlier, when students first begin writing papers referring to the works of others, the relevant material is not so closely tied within the research paper section that it cannot be assigned independently.

USING THE SECTION KEY

The Prentice-Hall Handbook for Writers provides an index section key inside the back cover of the text. This key makes it easy for you to refer a student to a particular section of the book. References to specific areas are indicated by section number. This arrangement aids the student in locating sections, since they are organized by numerical-alphabetical sequence, most sections being identified by large numbers at the top of text pages. Many instructors use abbreviations or correction symbols to indicate writing errors when grading student papers, and these abbreviations are also listed with the appropriate section in the key. Thus, students are given as much help as possible in finding those sections on which they need to concentrate. In addition, the end pages at the front of the text also list correction symbols, their explanations, and corresponding text sections.

An example of one way to use the index key is presented in the preface to the *Handbook*. It will be worth your while to spend a little time familiarizing yourself with the key. If you can become adept at using the numerical section references, you will save yourself many minutes of long, written explanations when grading student papers.

GLOSSARY OF USAGE AND AN INDEX TO GRAMMATICAL TERMS

While most students would probably protest being assigned the Glossary and Index to Terms for homework, these are valuable references, and you should familiarize yourself with them. You may wish to direct students to portions of these sections for definitions and explanations of terms and diction. As with the index key, the Glossary and Index to Terms can be turned into quick grading comments (for example: "See *could of*, 43").

THE TOTAL PRENTICE-HALL PACKAGE

As has been mentioned previously, the *Prentice-Hall Workbook for Writers* and the *Prentice-Hall Diagnostic Test* are companions to the *Handbook*. The *Workbook* provides succinct explanations and numerous exercises which correspond to the *Handbook's* sections. In addition, the *Workbook* is keyed by section to its parent text. The *Diagnostic Test* can be used effectively for placement and proficiency testing. The new second edition of the *Workbook* also contains several sections designed to provide practice or review for the *Diagnostic Test*. When used in combination, these three teaching tools can give you and your students a most complete fund of classroom materials.

SECTIONS 1-5

BASIC GRAMMAR

Grammar is an ugly word to many students. Their experiences
may have included mind-numbing drills or pedantically prescriptive
lists of rules which seemed to have little bearing on the realities
of spoken or written English. On the other hand, students may have
been influenced by teachers who thought free-flowing "expression"
to be more important than correct sentence construction. Still
others will have vague memories of grammar from junior high school,
but will have taken only literature courses since that time. And
you may also discover students who have studied "linguistics" but
have not been exposed to traditional grammar vocabulary or concepts.
A few will have had no type of formal grammar training at all.

Thus, faced with a variety of gruesome possibilities and almost certainly negative class attitudes, you would do well to emphasize the *Handbook's* introduction to the subject. Grammar is not
a set of arbitrary rules: it is "the system by which a language
works"--any language. Latin and lithography, cooking and computer
science all have their own distinct systems and languages for describing systematic relationships--their own grammars.

Hence, when individuals seek to communicate with one another,
they "speak" by means of a mutually comprehensible system. In our
case this is the grammar of English. Students frequently grasp the
idea of "mutual comprehensibility" as a logical rationale for the
need to master grammar, its concepts and vocabulary. In order to
discuss grammar, we need to understand a mutual vocabulary (words
like *noun, verb, clause,* etc.). In order to use grammar correctly,
we need to understand a common set of concepts (the functions the
vocabulary describes). The idea of "learning a language" in order
to talk about language often makes sense to students. After all,
they are asked to master new vocabularies and systems in biology,
economics, or math. Just because English is more or less their
"mother tongue," it need not be excluded from the same analytical
treatment.

And finally, of course, grammar is not an end in itself. It
is a tool for effective communication. An understanding of grammar
in no way insures overall good writing, but it is certainly a necessary building block for "mutually comprehensible" writing.

The use that can be made of sections 1-5 will quite obviously
depend on class proficiency in the aspects that are involved. With
more sophisticated students, you may not need to use the sections
for more than reference. Weaker students, on the other hand, may
profit from extended discussion of the sections and assignment of
the exercises.

The "Basic Grammar" Review Exercise at the end of these sections can be used as a test to determine the level of class

5

proficiency in the areas covered. If weaknesses are detected, additional exercises and assignments from the *Handbook* or the *Workbook* can provide extra practice and review.

SECTION 1

SENTENCE SENSE

A good craftsman knows his tools and the materials of his trade. How effectively he uses them involves his manipulative skills as an artisan; the more a cabinetmaker knows about the quality of his wood, the functions of his chisels, the dovetailing of a joint, the better able he is to build a table. If the table is to stand, the cabinetmaker must understand its parts and how these parts work together. Only then can he apply his tools and skill toward making them. Much the same is true of a writer, a craftsman in his own right. In the writer's case, the building materials are words. The ability to choose and manipulate words within different types of structures is his chief tool. The writer shows his skill at his craft when he obtains effective results.

Since the sentence is one of the basic structural devices a writer will work with, a good understanding of how it works is absolutely essential. Like the cabinetmaker, the writer must know its parts and how they work together before his sentence will stand. Thus he needs knowledge of parts of speech, verbals, phrases, clauses, and sentence patterns.

Section 1a emphasizes the basic sentence patterns: S V, S V O, and S V C. The emphasis here is primarily upon functioning of sentence elements rather than upon parts of speech as such. Function may be a new idea to students who often are used to simply locating the first noun in a sentence and calling it the subject. Function should be stressed, especially since the more familiar words *noun, verb, adjective*, etc. should also be seen in their functional capacities. You might begin by showing that sometimes a subject can take up practically all of a short sentence.

Doing exercises and maintaining regular hours helps one's health.

That he has been working too hard is evident.

Thus the subject is not necessarily just a noun: it is that part of the sentence which carries out the action of the verb or that part which the verb relates to the remainder of the sentence.

In section 1b, which deals with parts of speech, students often have trouble with verbals, adjectives, and adverbs. Verbal problems can be lessened if students understand the functions of the three types: infinitives, participles, and gerunds. They need to learn that none of these can ever fulfill the functions of verbs in sentences, even though they are based on verb stems and look like verb forms. Confusing verbs and verbals is a common cause of sentence fragments in students' writing.

7

Another troublesome area is adverbs and adjectives. You may need to emphasize that only adverbs can modify adjectives: *really good movie* instead of *real good movie*. Contexts involving linking verbs used in a *seem* or *appear* sense can also cause problems. The linking verb acts as an equal sign and connects the subject to its predicate modifier--which must be an adjective (not an adverb), because only adjectives may modify the nouns or noun substitutes that form the subject. Perhaps such an explanation will cure your students' inclination to write *He feels badly* instead of *He feels bad*.

You will probably also want to direct students' attention to section 1b(5), which notes that some words can be either adverbs or prepositions. When used as adverbs, words like *down, out,* and *below* never have objects.

Sections 1c and 1d discuss phrases and clauses, components crucial to understanding the main and subordinate elements of a sentence, and hence to achieving greater sentence emphasis and variety. Students often confuse phrases and clauses, so a careful study of the distinguishing features and functions of each is usually time well spent. Again, emphasis on infinitive, participle, and gerund phrases may help eliminate sentence fragments in compositions.

Exercises 1d(1) and 1d(3) stress not only clause recognition but also clause function. You will want to be sure your students understand that a grammatical construction has a purpose within a sentence. When they see that a subordinate clause, for example, may act as an adjective, adverb, or noun, they are on their way to a stronger perception of the way language works.

Exercise 1a

You may wish to limit identification of predicate parts to main clauses. For the convenience of those who do not, however, verbs, objects, and predicate nouns of subordinate clauses are also indicated. You may also want your students to identify the subject in each sentence as well. Sentence patterns are indicated after each sentence in the order in which the sentence patterns occur.

```
        V      PN
1.  War is a disease.  Pattern 5.

                V
2.  The geese circled slowly.  Pattern 1

                     V        DO
3.  Recent studies prove the dangers of cigarettes.  Pattern 2

                            V
4.  To be useful, a dictionary must be used.  Passive Sentence

              V   IO       DO              V
5.  His friends gave Sam a reception when he returned.  Patterns
    4, 1
```

```
                      V           IO                DO
6.  Local citizens sent the police many complaints about burglaries
    in the neighborhood.  Pattern 4

                   V           DO
7.  Poverty deprives many children of an education.  Pattern 2

                        V
8.  The blue Buick raced down the narrow road.  Pattern 1

                          V   IO      DO
9.  Television and radio bring us the news daily.  Pattern 4

                                        V          DO
10. People who live in glass houses shouldn't throw stones.
    Pattern 2
```

Exercise 1b

The following exercise answers use traditional terminology for
the classification of parts of speech. Instructors who prefer more
recent word classifications will want to make some changes in the
answers suggested, and the text, together with the glossary, provides basic information on inflectional endings and the like. It
may also be appropriate to call students' attention to some terms
(e.g., *expletive, article, demonstrative adjective, adjectival* or
possessive pronouns) which appear in the glossary or at subsequent
points in the text. Note that *her* in sentence 8 and *his* in sentences 9 and 10 below are pronouns used as adjectives.

```
        art   noun    verb  prep art    noun
1.  The blizzard raged from the northeast.

        int   pron    verb     adj   noun    adv
2.  Stop!  I 've heard that excuse before.

        noun       verb    conj   noun    verb pron pron    verb
3.  Pollution increases though scientists warn that  it   threatens

    pron   noun
    our  survival.

        noun        noun     conj noun  verb art adv     adj
4.  Newspapers, magazines, and  books are  the most powerful

     noun     prep      noun
    weapons against ignorance.

    art  noun   prep  adj    noun   verb   adv      adj     prep
5.  The streets  of  seaside resorts are strangely desolate  in

     noun
    winter.

     gerund      noun    verb art  adj    adj    noun    prep
6.  Misreading directions  is   a  common student mistake  in

    gerund      noun
    taking examinations.
```

```
        adj  noun  verb   adj     adv art noun    verb      pron
7.  That cave  is    unsafe;  even the bats have left   it.

    noun adv    verb    prep pron adj    noun
8.  Sally soon recovered from her  severe injuries.

        noun    verb pron art noun verb prep art noun adv  adj  conj
9.  Einstein said that  a  man  has  at  the most only two   or

    adj  noun  prep pron   noun
    three ideas  in  his  lifetime.

    art noun  verb   adv  verb pron adj  noun conj pron verb adv
10.  A  man  should never wear his  best suit when  he  goes out

     inf    prep  noun   conj noun
    to fight for  freedom and  truth.
```

Exercise 1c

1. Both little girls and little boys dream <u>of becoming astronauts</u>.

2. <u>Watching football</u> <u>on TV</u> is the favorite sport <u>of millions</u>.

3. Language is the most amazing invention <u>of man</u>.

4. <u>After working late into the night</u>, Mary went to bed.

5. The tornado struck the town, <u>ripping roofs</u> <u>from houses</u>, <u>wrenching trees</u> <u>from the ground</u>.

6. Smith wanted <u>to hold</u> the foreman <u>to his promise</u>.

7. <u>For many years</u> the gap <u>between the rich and the poor in South America</u> has been widening.

8. <u>Being loyal</u> <u>to her principles</u> was more important <u>to Jane</u> than <u>gaining approval</u> <u>from her friends</u>.

9. <u>Rising in a graceful arc</u>, the space ship swung <u>into orbit</u>.

10. Reports <u>of flying saucers</u> grew frequent <u>in the summer</u>.

Exercise 1d(1)

```
                               adv
1.  We tried our new speedboat when the sea was calm.

                 adj
2.  The apples that make the best pies are the sour ones.

                            adv
3.  She enrolled in college because she wanted to be a lawyer.

            noun
4.  What annoyed him was the clerk's indifference.

         adv
5.  While he was telephoning, the doorbell rang.

                                 noun
6.  Many parents think that education is to be gotten only
    in school.
```

```
                   noun
7.  What one thinks at twenty often seems silly at thirty.

                               adv
8.  Many would be rich if success depended only on work.

                                     adj
9.  She had the quality of innocence that the director needed.

                adv
10. We left before the movie was over.
```

Exercise 1d(2)

```
    SC(adv)                        MC
1.  As the class ended, the teacher sighed with relief.

                MC                          SC(adj)
2.  Many of the unemployed lack the skills that they need for jobs

3.  One objection to capital punishment is that it is inconsis-
    tently administered.
    Entire sentence is the main clause.

                MC                      SC(adj)
4.  The ideal summer job is one which involves little work and
    much money.
                MC                      SC(adv)
5.  A clause is subordinate if it serves as a single part of speech

                     SC(adj)
6.  The price that John wanted for his car was too high.
    "The price was too high" is the main clause.

                 SC(adv)                     MC
7.  If marijuana is not addictive, why shouldn't it be legal?

                MC                          SC(adj)
8.  An educated person is one who knows not only the extent

    of his knowledge but also its limits.
                                       SC(noun)
9.  Some parents let their children do whatever they please.
    Entire sentence is main clause.
                                    SC(noun)
10. The most valuable of all talents is that of never using

    two words where one will do.
    Entire sentence is main clause.  Subordinate clause
    beginning with that acts as noun complement.
```

Exercise 1d(3)

```
1.  Simple              6.  Compound-Complex
2.  Compound            7.  Compound
3.  Complex             8.  Simple
4.  Compound            9.  Complex
5.  Compound-Complex   10.  Complex
```

SECTION 2

CASE

Case is not something that ordinarily will have to be emphasized a great deal, since case is not nearly as important an aspect of the English language as it is of other languages. There are some types of troublesome constructions involving case, however, that you may desire to stress. The possessive case of the personal pronoun, *it*, for example, is very frequently misspelled as *it's* instead of *its*. Therefore, as case is discussed, it might be desirable to draw attention to this fact in the hope of avoiding in the future at least one common spelling error.

Two constructions which are particularly troublesome and which, for that reason, should be specifically discussed are those involving a pronoun that is the subject of a clause which functions as the object of a verb or preposition, and a noun or pronoun preceding a gerund. In this connection, sentences of the type, *Who do you think is right?* are frequently written incorrectly as *Whom do you think is right?* and sentences of the type *I know nothing of his being there* are frequently written incorrectly as *I know nothing of him being there.*

Two types of constructions in which informal expressions seem very close to acceptance at the formal level are those discussed in sections 2b and 2c. Here, you will probably want to exercise independent judgment and decide for yourself whether expressions such as *I thought it was him* will be acceptable in lieu of *I thought it was he.* You may also want to accept expressions such as *It is me* instead of *It is I.* Technically, only the latter expressions above are acceptable in formal writing. In actual practice, however, more and more of the informal usages above seem to be creeping into what is generally regarded as formal writing.

Exercise 2

Some portions of exercises 2 through 5 deal with problems in which formal and informal usage frequently differ. Answers suggested follow conservative usage. You may, of course, allow for more informal choices when appropriate. Where dictionaries record alternative verb forms, both have been cited.

1. He has lived in Cleveland longer than *I*. (The pronoun *I* is the subject of the understood verb *have*.)

2. It was *she* who was elected to the student council. (Nominative case of personal pronoun, *she*, is required after linking verb *was*.)

3. When we heard the footsteps, we knew it was *he*. (Nominative case of personal pronoun, *he*, is required after linking verb *was*.)

13

4. I appreciate soul music without *his* telling me what to listen for. (The possessive form of the adjectival pronoun is required to modify the gerund.)

5. They considered the logical candidate to be *me*. *(Me* is the object of the infinitive *to be.)*

6. We found Mark and *her* in the swimming pool. *(Her* is the object of the verb *found.)*

7. The teacher reported Dick as well as *me* for cheating. *(Me* is the object of the verb *reported.)*

8. Burgess was the candidate *whom* all educated people voted for. (The relative pronoun *whom* is the object of the preposition *for.)*

9. We will consider *whoever* applies for it. *(Whoever* is the subject of the verb *applies* in the subordinate clause *whoever applies for it.)*

10. There was no reason for *my* staying any longer. (The possessive form *my* is required before the gerund.)

TENSE AND MOOD

Using the various verb tenses is often easier than explaining them, and if your class exhibits only minor problems with tense, you may be tempted to leave well enough alone. However, it is quite possible that your students have relied on "playing it by ear" and have never really worked through the rationale behind verb usage. Additionally, some of your students may have trouble with correct usage because the speech of their minority group ignores or mutates some forms in some tenses. Consequently, a thorough study of verb tense and mood should not be avoided unless you are quite sure it is not necessary. Although students may infrequently need perfect and progressive forms, they will undoubtedly benefit from a knowledge of their uses and functions. If, on the other hand, the class has basic verb problems with simple tenses and plain forms, you may want to wait until a later class period to tackle the complexities of more sophisticated verb usage.

Before assigning section 3 of the text, you should probably introduce the class to the material yourself, perhaps through a combination of lecture and discussion. If students are unsure about verb tenses, reading the text alone will most likely frighten and confuse them. The whole subject will be too forbidding. For example, you could begin by establishing the function of verbs in general: to show action, condition, or state of being; and equally important, to establish the time frame in which the action or condition occurs: present, past, or future. Students have less trouble handling tense if they remember it is the principal key to time in a sentence.

Following that beginning definition, you can distinguish between regular and irregular verbs. Sometimes a little etymology or language history helps a class see why some verbs form their past tense by adding -d, -ed while others require a vowel shift, as in *drive, drove, driven.* Anything you can do to dispel the mystery surrounding verbs will help students' retention; bits of trivia and explanation often make the subject more accessible for them.

A review of principal parts could be your next step (hitting the most frequently abused ones: see the text, pp. 35-37), followed by a careful exploration of all the tenses. The *Handbook's* definitions on pages 33-34 should be quite helpful here. After this, you will want to explore the progressive form of verbs, something most students have never heard of. The *Prentice-Hall Workbook* contains a thorough discussion of progressive verb forms, and you may wish to assign those sections or use them for examples.

The *Handbook* provides a useful paradigm of the regular and irregular verbs "ask" and "drive" on page 34. This paradigm illustrates both active and passive voice. Since many students have no knowledge of the passive voice, although they may use it in speaking and writing, you will want to be sure they understand its

15

purpose and forms. In fact, it may be necessary to provide more detail than is available in the *Handbook* and more examples.

One way to stimulate an in-class probe of verb tense is to select a verb such as "drag" and ask students to form a sentence which correctly expresses in tense, form, and voice a condition that you prescribe. For example, you can ask for a sentence in the first person which expresses future action: "I will drag myself out of bed tomorrow." Or a sentence that indicates the action is in the process of being completed right now: "I am dragging myself out of bed." Once students have become proficient in the active voice, you can ask for passive verbs: "I am being dragged out of bed by the ringing of my alarm clock."

The point that verb tenses allow us to be quite specific about actions or conditions placed in time should be your focus. The following explanations may help you get this across to them.

ACTIVE VOICE

PRESENT: "I *drag* a sled" means I perform this action regularly although I may not be doing it now. By comparison, "I *am dragging* a sled" (progressive form) means that I am presently engaged in such a process.

PAST: "Yesterday at noon I *dragged* a sled" means either I dragged a sled at that particular time or I was in the business of dragging sleds, although I may or may not have been performing that specific action at that time. By comparison, if I want to indicate that at a certain time I was dragging a sled, I would probably say: "Yesterday at noon I *was dragging* a sled" (progressive form).

FUTURE: "Tomorrow at noon I *shall drag* a sled" means that I will start the action at that time. "Tomorrow at noon I *shall be dragging* a sled" means, by comparison, that I will have already started the action as of the time indicated.

If, on the other hand, I want to speak of an action I have completed after the present but less remotely in the future than a specified time, I can say "Tomorrow at noon I *shall have dragged* a sled," whereas if I want to deal with an action that has started and is still continuing at a future time, I can say "Tomorrow at noon I *shall have been dragging* a sled."

PAST PERFECT VS. PRESENT PERFECT: "Yesterday at noon I *had dragged* a sled" means that with respect to a past time prior to another past time, I had taken such an action. By comparison, "I *have dragged* a sled" means that sometime in the past with respect to the present time, I have taken such an action. Such an expression may also imply that the past action is one that is continuing up to the present, although an even stronger way of indicating such a continuing action would be to say "I *have been dragging* a sled."

The only mood that may give students trouble is the subjunctive. Because the subjunctive is seldom used, except for sentences expressing contrary-to-fact condition, you may have difficulty explaining its appropriateness. This is especially true since some informal expressions are on the verge of respectability, and it will frequently be a matter of judgment as to whether you accept "The elm tree looks as if it was dying" in lieu of "The elm tree looks as if it were dying." By the same token, expressions such as "I wish that I was taller" are appearing more regularly in good writing. As a result, you will have to decide for yourself the degree of formality you will require in students' compositions and exercise answers. The exercise answers provided for 3e-g below follow conservative formal usage.

Exercise 3a-d

1. The trash *lay* on the office floor for days. *(Lay* is past tense of verb *lie.)*

2. Plans for the space launch were *begun* in the spring. (Past participle of verb *begin* is used to form passive voice of the verb.)

3. Soon after the fire started, rats *came* rushing out of the basement. *(Came* is the past tense of *come*; note that its formation is irregular.)

4. The spy denied that he had *stolen* the blueprints. (Past participle of the verb *steal* is required, along with the appropriate auxiliary verb *had* to form the past perfect tense.)

5. My new bikini *shrunk, shrank* when it was washed. *(Webster's New World Dictionary of the American Language* gives both *shrunk* and *shrank* as acceptable for past tense of verb *shrink.)*

6. He was *prejudiced* against the city because he had always *lived* on a farm. (Past participles of verbs *prejudice* and *live* are required to form past passive and past perfect tenses.)

7. On its first trial, the new speedboat has *broken* the record. (Past participle of verb *break* and the auxiliary *has* are required to form the present perfect tense.)

8. I would have liked *to see* Garbo in the movies. (The present infinitive is required after the perfect tense verb *have liked.)*

9. If he *had tried,* he *could have avoided* skidding off the road. (The tense of the verb in the subordinate clause must be compatible with the tense of the verb in the main clause.)

10. When I got home, I found I had *torn* my new jacket. (The past participle of *tear* is required, along with the auxiliary to form the past perfect tense.)

17

Exercise 3e-g

1. After the crash, the injured *were lying* all over the highway. (*Were lying* is the correct participial form of the verb *lie.*)

2. The *Titanic* was considered unsinkable, but it *sank, sunk* in a few hours. (*Sank* is the standard past tense of *sink*, but many dictionaries also list *sunk* as an alternative past tense.)

3. Roosevelt *led* the nation through some difficult times. (Students frequently misspell the past tense of *lead.*)

4. The revolution might have succeeded, if people *had been* ready to fight. (This sentence requires not only the past perfect subjunctive but also tense compatibility between subordinate and main clauses.)

5. Any one would be happier if he *were* a millionaire. (Contrary-to-fact condition expressed in this sentence requires the use of the subjunctive mood.)

6. I won't invite them because they *drank* too much at my last party. (*Webster's New World Dictionary* regards *drunk* in the past tense as archaic; however, *drunk* as it is used in the above sentence would still probably be acceptable in many colloquial situations.)

7. World peace would be assured if all nations *sat* down together and talked. (*Set* is unacceptable here, even in informal language.)

8. The president demands that Jane *resign* her position. (The use of a "formal demand" indicates the necessity for the subjunctive mood in this sentence.)

9. Both Jake and I *swam* across the lake and back. (*Swum*, according to most dictionaries, is the archaic past tense of *swim*; it might be acceptable in some colloquial speech, but hardly in formal writing.)

10. Had I *known* I could *ride*, I would have *gone*. (*Know* is an irregular verb and thus cannot form its past and perfect tenses with -*ed*. The use of the perfect tense, *had known* requires the present tense *ride*. The auxiliary *have* requires the past participle *gone.*)

SECTION 4

ADJECTIVES AND ADVERBS

A solid knowledge of the parts of speech is the best remedy for adjective and adverb troubles. If students are weak in this area, you may want them to review section 1b in the *Handbook*: an adjective qualifies the meaning of a noun or pronoun, an adverb qualifies the meaning of a verb, adjective, or another adverb. Section 4 uses negative examples and corrected versions to clarify the uses of both types of modifiers.

You may also discover that students who know the difference between an adjective and an adverb habitually forget to add *-ly* endings to adverbs when they write. This is probably because informal speech frequently drops the *-ly*. One method for correcting this habit is to prepare a series of sentences for which students must supply modifiers in either the adjectival or adverbial form, adding or dropping the *-ly* as necessary. The *Prentice-Hall Workbook* contains exercises of this type, if you do not wish to construct your own.

As in section 1, adjectives with linking verbs are likely to need special attention. In addition, the comparative and superlative forms of adjectives and adverbs sometimes cause difficulty because of students' tendencies to use the superlative instead of the comparative form when comparing only two as in *Ruth was the most athletic of the two*. Certain words (such as *good, bad,* and *delicious*) which are compared in an irregular manner also cause some confusion. A good recommendation is that students refer to one of the better desk dictionaries when in doubt. Dictionaries list comparative and superlative forms that are irregular.

Exercise 4

1. Student leaders must take their obligations more *seriously*. (*Seriously* modifies the verb *take*.)

2. I felt very *bad* about not seeing him. (Because *felt* is a linking verb, the adjective *bad* should be used after it. *Badly* is a colloquial usage.)

3. The South Pole is the *colder* of the two Poles. (Because only two are being compared, *coldest* would be incorrect.)

4. John is the *taller* of the two brothers. (Only two are being compared.)

5. Our society is based on the belief that all men are created *equal*. (The emphasis here is on the status of equality, not on the process of being created; hence, the adjective *equal* is preferable to the adverb *equally*.)

19

6. Owls can see *well* at night. (The modifier refers to the verb *see*; hence, the adverb *well* rather than the adjective *good* should be used.)

7. Would a rose by any other name smell as *sweet?* (The linking verb *smell* requires the adjective *sweet*; the emphasis is on the effect the rose produces, not upon how it itself performs the action of smelling.)

8. At first even the critics didn't understand *Lolita* because it is a *unique* book. (*Unique* is "absolute" in its meaning and thus should not be further qualified or modified, although in informal speech *very unique* may be acceptable.)

9. The accident was not *nearly* as bad as it would have been if he had not been driving *slowly*. (The adverb *nearly* in conjunction with *as* modifies the adjective *bad*; adverb *slowly* modifies the verb *had been driving.*)

10. The tall ships sailed *majestically* into the harbor. (An adverbial modifier is necessary; *majestically* explains <u>how</u> the ships *sailed.*)

DIAGRAMING GRAMMATICAL RELATIONSHIPS

Although diagraming is not as extensively employed as it once was, the *Handbook* includes a section for those who like to use it as an instructional aid. The text provides a number of examples and exercises, covering most of the basic structural situations you may want to illustrate.

As the title of the section indicates, diagraming is particularly good for showing relationships among parts of sentences: that noun clauses, gerund phrases, and infinitive phrases can act as complements, subjects, and objects, for example. Diagraming can also help students grasp the difference between prepositional phrases and infinitives. It can also illustrate the function of the participial phrase, thus helping to eliminate participial sentence fragments in compositions.

If you have been emphasizing grammatical function, as this manual suggests, you may find diagraming a surprisingly effective graphic means of establishing many functional relationships. Students need not be capable of elaborate diagraming techniques themselves to follow you through a "chalk-talk" of illustrative diagramed examples.

Exercise 5(1)

1. Life | is \ short.

2. Russia | invaded | Czechoslovakia.

3. Marijuana | offered | escape.
          \ them

4. floodwaters | overflowed | riverbank.
   The \ rising   the

5. regulations | irritated | students.
   The \ outdated   severely   the

Exercise 5(2)

1. *Balancing the national budget* is a gerund phrase used as a
    subject and should go on stilts *above* the base line.

2. *With questions* is a prepositional phrase modifying *besieged*.
    It should go *beneath* the base line.

3. *To marry well and (to) retire soon* are infinitive phrases
    which should be placed on stilts *above* the base line.

4. *Hunting for antiques* is a gerund complement which includes the
    modifying prepositional phrase *for antiques*. Hence, the con-
    struction goes on stilts *above* the base line.

5. *To ignore others' misery* is an infinitive phrase used as a
    subject; *to aggravate it* is an infinitive phrase used as a
    complement. Both should go *above* the base line on stilts.

Exercise 5(3)

1. *That it has little power* is the complement of the verb *is* and
    should be placed *above* the base line.

2. *Toward which both communism and capitalism are moving* modifies
    economy and should be placed *below* the base line.

3. *That their demands were nonnegotiable* is the object of the
    verb *insisted* and should be placed *above* the base line.

4. The sentence is compound, having two main clauses: *The
    continent of Africa is now divided into nations* on one base
    line should be separated from *tribal divisions are more faith-
    fully observed* on another base line by a step line on which
    but is underlined.

5. *That violence is not a viable alternative* is a complement and
    should be placed *above* the line.

"Basic Grammar" Review Exercise

(Sections 1 through 5))

1. If Judy *were* coming home tomorrow, I would not leave today.
    (Subjunctive mood is required because a condition contrary to
    fact is involved.)

2. Cleveland was the first major city that *had* a black mayor.
    (The tense of the verb *have* must be consistent with the tense
    of the verb *was*; hence *had* is required.)

3. Many policemen feel *bad* over reports of police brutality.
    (The linking verb *feel* requires an adjective rather than an
    adverb.)

4. After the play ended, the cast *appeared* for curtain calls.
    (The past tense, *appeared*, is necessary for consistency with

ended. (The entire sentence might also be cast in the present tense.)

5. That snake looks as if he *were* getting ready to strike. (Contrary-to-fact condition requires the subjunctive in formal usage.)

6. The boxer *saw* at once that his opponent was a harder puncher than *he.* (The past tense of *see*, rather than the past participle, is needed in this sentence. The pronoun *he* should be in the nominative case in formal English, as it is the subject of the understood verb *was.*)

7. It was *he* and not I who forgot the date. (The nominative case of the personal pronoun is used after forms of the verb *be* in formal English.)

8. International relations may improve greatly if China and the United States *establish* diplomatic relations. (The tense sequence requires the present, *establish*, rather than the past, *established.*)

9. She did not say it was I *whom* she wanted to see. (*Whom* is the object of the verb phrase *wanted to see* and thus must be in the objective case.)

10. After the war ended, everyone *began* making plans for the next one. (Internal consistency between clauses requires that the past tense be used. Alternatively, the verbs in both clauses could be written in the present tense.)

11. His sister works *considerably* harder than he does. (*Harder* is an adverb and thus may only be modified by another adverb: *considerably.*)

12. NASA was *surely* delighted when the space shot proceeded on schedule. (The adverbial form must be used to modify the verb phrase *was delighted.*)

13. It *would have been interesting to watch* a debate between Eisenhower and Stevenson. (Present tense infinitive is correct after a verb in the perfect tense.)

14. All of *us* recent employees must attend orientation meetings. (The objective case of the pronoun is necessary as *us* is the object of the preposition *of.*)

15. All families were prepared when the blizzard *struck.* (*Struck* is the past tense of *strike* and is required for consistency with the past tense passive voice verb *were prepared.*)

BASIC SENTENCE FAULTS

Errors in basic sentence structure can impart an air of near illiteracy to a student's writing. Sometimes you will discover that students repeatedly write fragments and fused sentences because they really do not understand what a sentence is: their grasp of sentence components and parts of speech is so poor that they cannot identify a subject or a verb. If this is the case, a review of section 1 is in order before any headway can be made.

Other students write faulty sentences mainly through carelessness. There are two or three in every class who end a sentence wherever they have paused to phrase the next group of words--no matter whether a period is appropriate or not. Similarly, you may find students who join thought after thought with commas, regardless of the independent clauses in between. For these students, drills requiring them to underline every independent clause and label every subject and verb in their writing can help them distinguish between word groups that are sentences and word groups that are not.

Correct sentence structure is also basic to coherence. At a more sophisticated level of writing, many students, in the attempt to achieve smooth thought flow between sentences and paragraphs, will experience difficulty with coherence. But poorly written, flawed sentences are even more fatal to coherence than the failure to establish sentence relationships; if individual sentences are good, the reader has at least a fighting chance to impose an integrated meaning upon them. If the reader has trouble getting through the sentences themselves, his or her task becomes a nearly impossible one.

SECTION 6

SENTENCE FRAGMENT

Students write sentence fragments because they either fail to include a verb (sometimes a subject is also left out) or they fail to realize that certain constructions are subordinate and must have a related main clause before the constructions become sentences. The failure to include verbs often occurs because the student mistakes a participle in a construction for a verb as in *His reason for not going being his sore leg. Being,* a participle, in the previous construction looks like a verb but isn't one. If students experience trouble in this area, it might be worth the time to elaborate a little upon the difference between the progressive form of the verb *be, being,* and the participle *being.* If they can be made to understand the difference in function between the participle and progressive forms of verbs, students will write fewer fragments.

Students having spent time on section 1d, "Recognizing Clauses," should be able to identify subordinate clauses and should not write a subordinate construction as a sentence. If trouble still persists in this area, Exercise 6, which requires the combining of subordinate elements with independent elements, should help. Another approach would be to discuss the various subordinating conjunctions (*when, if, as, since, because,* etc.), stressing that where these words head a clause, a subordinate clause is present and, hence, an independent clause must also be present before the sentence is complete.

Exercise 6

Many other variations are of course possible when revising these sentences. In particular, you may wish to emphasize noun clauses by placing subordinate clauses first in the first sentence revisions of 2, 4, 5, 6, 9, and 10.

1. The two candidates have the same plans, the only difference being their party. *OR* The two candidates have the same plans. The only difference is their party.

2. Carter's first budget was one of the largest in history, even though he had promised to cut it. *OR* Carter's first budget was one of the largest in history. Such was the case even though he had promised to cut it.

3. Many young people consider social work as a career--not for the money, but for the satisfaction it provides. *OR* Many young people consider social work as a career. They consider it not for the money, but for the satisfaction it provides.

4. The Beatles decided to stop giving concerts just as they were at the peak of their form. *OR* The Beatles decided to stop giving concerts. They did so just as they were at the peak of their form.

25

5. Violence has become a tool of political dissent chiefly be-
    cause nonviolence can be so easily ignored. *OR* Violence has
    become a tool of political dissent. Such is true because non-
    violence can be so easily ignored.

6. He visited Tuesday afternoon immediately after he had arrived
    from Los Angeles. *OR* He visited Tuesday afternoon. His
    visit began immediately after he had arrived from Los Angeles.

7. I think we should ignore their insults or leave quickly. *OR*
    I think we should ignore their insults. Otherwise, we should
    leave quickly.

8. Linda has saved $700, enough to make a down payment on a car.
    OR Linda has saved $700. This sum is enough to make a down
    payment on a car.

9. Congress has investigated the Kennedy assassination many
    times trying to determine whether there was a conspiracy. *OR*
    Congress has investigated the Kennedy assassination several
    times. Its investigations have tried to determine whether
    there was a conspiracy.

10. Many doctors refuse to prescribe birth control pills because
    some women have serious side effects from them. *OR* Many
    doctors refuse to prescribe birth control pills. Their
    reason is that some women have serious side effects from them.

    In 2, 4, 5, 6, 9, and 10 above, the dependent clause can be
located at the beginning of the sentence. There are of course
additional variations in the ways these sentences can be written.

COMMA SPLICE AND RUN-TOGETHER OR FUSED SENTENCE

When your class is studying the fused sentence (or run-on), you can also tackle the semicolon. Semicolons seem to be a perennial mystery, and the students who love them best are often those who use them least correctly. As one experienced professor remarked to her freshmen, "You can live your whole life without the semicolon--try it." Nevertheless, students initiated into the cult of the semicolon sprinkle it liberally throughout their writing, apparently finding it a more sophisticated punctuation mark then the mundane period.

The most you can do is get them to place it correctly: between independent clauses not linked by coordinating conjunctions and before clauses introduced by conjunctive adverbs such as *however*, *consequently*, *therefore*, etc. Once a student understands that a semicolon can be used between independent elements, he or she may be able to resist the temptation to write comma splices. It is worth mentioning, however, that semicolons are most effective when they separate independent elements that have a close thought-content relationship (a logical reason, in fact, for using the semicolon with conjunctive adverbs).

In a similar vein, achieving a knowledge of subordinating conjunctions such as *after*, *when*, and *because* can help students avoid run-on sentences and comma splices created by "jamming" too many independent elements together.

Exercise 7

In this exercise, two sample answers are given. One involves the use of the semicolon; the other involves subordinating parts of the sentence. Generally other ways of rewriting the sentences are possible. In some instances, for example, a colon or dash could be employed instead of a semicolon. In other cases, separating the original sentence into two sentences would be possible.

1. The automobile crashed headlong into the wall; then all was quiet. *OR* After the automobile crashed headlong into the wall, all was quiet.

2. The best way to publicize a movie is to say it's "For Adults Only"; then everyone will flock to see it. *OR* If a movie is publicized as being "For Adults Only," then everyone will flock to see it.

3. After the blood transfusion, the patient was comfortable; so the doctor left for coffee. *OR* Since the patient was comfortable after the blood transfusion, the doctor left for coffee.

4. My brother must be color blind; he calls all colors blue. *OR* Since he calls all colors blue, my brother must be color blind.

5. Eisenhower wrote a book about World War II; he called it *Crusade in Europe*. *OR* Eisenhower wrote a book, *Crusade in Europe*, about World War II.

6. Population continues to increase in most of the world; we will soon not have enough food for all. *OR* Since population continues to increase in most of the world, we will soon not have enough food for all.

7. Most of Hemingway's novels have similar subjects; love and war are two of the most frequent. *OR* Most of Hemingway's novels have similar subjects, love and war being two of the most frequent.

8. Water is becoming scarce in many parts of the country; our children may have to ration it. *OR* Since water is becoming scarce in many parts of the country, our children may have to ration it.

9. Russia and China were close allies for many years; however, they are now very suspicious of each other. *OR* Although Russia and China were close allies for many years, they are now very suspicious of each other.

10. We are never challenged by television; it's much easier to watch the screen than to read a book. *OR* We are never challenged by television because it's much easier to watch the screen than to read a book.

FAULTY AGREEMENT AND FAULTY REFERENCE OF PRONOUNS

All of us make agreement errors, even though we may know better. Subject-verb agreement usually goes awry when modifiers or prepositional phrases intervene or when subjects are compound. Faulty noun-pronoun agreement can occur in the same way. Faulty pronoun reference frequently involves the vague and indefinite use of *this, that, which, they, you,* and *it.* For this reason you may particularly wish to emphasize sections 9c, d, and e.

Student writing also exhibits vague pronoun reference when pronouns are introduced too far from their antecedents, and especially when several other nouns have appeared between an antecedent and its referring pronoun. Encourage your students to use the noun or a synonym instead of pronoun if the reader is apt to become confused by a "latent" pronoun, or if there are two possible antecedents for a pronoun (see sections 9a and b).

"Everyone ... they" is a habitual error because in informal speech we usually forget to use the singular pronoun. Students may remember that formal usage requires the singular if you tell them to take their cue from the last half of the compound: "one" and "body" (as in *someone, everybody, anyone*) are obviously singular, regardless of what "some," "every," and "any" suggest.

As elementary as faulty agreement and reference may be--and as often as students have surely heard the material repeated-- annoying agreement and reference errors will continue to surface in most of the compositions you grade. Though the class may moan, direct assignments or class discussions of the exercises in these sections are probably wise.

Exercise 8a

1. His only interest *is* his studies.

2. A fool and his money *are* soon parted.

3. Among my favorite books *is Nine Stories* by Salinger.

4. The burden of sales taxes *falls* on the poor.

5. Taste in movies *differs* greatly.

6. Neither of the leaders *was* certain of popular support.

7. The farmer, and not the city dweller, *is* hurt when food prices fall.

8. Twenty dollars *is* more than many can afford for a pair of shoes.

29

9. He is one of those candidates who *do* not take a stand on specific issues.

10. There *are* a good many reasons for tension between Arabs and Israelis.

Exercise 8b

1. A person should be willing to defend *his(her)* own principles.

2. Neither of the leaders was willing to compromise on *his(her)* demands.

3. Every American should be free to live wherever *he(she)* can afford.

4. The Kennedy family has carried on in spite of *its* tragedies.

5. Everybody has *his(her)* own solution to the race problem.

6. None of the students in the psychology class could analyze *his(her)* own dreams.

7. If either a black woman or a white woman were qualified, *she* would get the job.

8. No child appreciates *his(her)* parents until later in life.

9. The school board disagreed in *their* opinions about closing the Adams school.

10. The citizens' group submitted *its* report to the mayor.

Exercise 8c

1. Poverty is one of the major forces that *encourages* crime.

2. If someone wants to "do *his(her)* thing," *he(she)* should be allowed to.

3. These *sorts* of planes can exceed the speed of sound.

4. Congress should pass a law that everyone must vote or *(he/she)* will be fined.

5. The President, with his cabinet members, *is* touring South America.

6. Two solutions to national traffic problems have been offered, but neither *has* been tried.

7. After thirty, one loses both the rebelliousness and the inventiveness of *his(her)* earlier years.

8. Although everyone wants the right to vote, *he(she)* doesn't always exercise that right at election time.

9. If world peace is to be assured, either the Eastern bloc or the Western bloc must alter *its* position.

10. The committee on admission of new members *does* not approve the nomination of Mr. Smith.

Exercise 9a

Most of the items in the exercises from this point through section 14 require revision. However, in most instances, there is no one "right" answer. Consequently, suggested revisions are only representative. Perhaps the most important thing is that the student learn to recognize the various ways to approach grammatically incorrect, awkward, or obscure sentences. Ideally, the student will sense that how he or she is to revise will depend upon the larger context (*e.g.*, emphasis, transition). In many of the exercises, you may want the student to suggest more than one way of revision. Another approach might be to require the student to defend a particular revision with reference to a larger context.

1. Kathy was very angry when she visited her mother. *OR* Her mother was very angry when Kathy visited her.

2. George had a dog which was always scratching fleas. *OR* George's dog was always scratching fleas.

3. Dad told Ross, "You stayed up watching television too late." *OR* Dad told Ross, "I stayed up watching television too late."

4. He painted the shutters after he took them off the window frames. *OR* After he took the shutters off, he painted the window frame.

5. Take the baby out and then throw the bath water away. *OR* After you have taken the baby out, throw the bath water away.

6. He broke the record when he dropped the phonograph arm on it. *OR* The phonograph arm broke when he dropped it on the record.

7. Sidney gave his brother a copy of one of the latter's favorite books, *Catcher in the Rye*. *OR* Sidney's favorite book was *Catcher in the Rye*, a copy of which he gave to his brother.

8. The American people have elected several inadequate Presidents, but Congress had kept such Presidents from ruining the country. *OR* Congress has kept the several inadequate Presidents which the American people have elected from ruining the country.

9. If Hitler had behaved differently with Stalin, the latter (Stalin) might not have had to take the action he did. *OR* If Hitler had behaved differently with Stalin, the former (Hitler) might not have had to take the action he did.

10. Marilyn told Susan "I(you) should never have married Jim." *OR* Marilyn told Susan the former (the latter) should never have married Jim.

Exercise 9b

1. The school belongs to the community. It could be the meeting place for all community activities. Students and their parents should work closely with faculty and administrators in developing programs for instruction and recreation.

2. The delegates arrived in twos and threes for the emergency session at the U.N. They stopped only to pose for the press photographers at the entrance. Interested spectators were also streaming in.

3. As the computer projected the election returns, the crowd watched and moaned and groaned. The defeat was unexpected.

4. He argued that artists, writers, and even office workers find it necessary to use marijuana as a means of relaxation.

5. He and his opponent made promises to the people of the nation to augment and revitalize the various poverty programs. But such promises were soon forgotten after the election.

Exercise 9c

1. The limited aid to Third World countries angered many blacks in South Africa.

2. On election day, people should always vote as an indication of their desire to have good government.

3. A part of the museum on the south side is open to the public.

4. Her real friends weren't bothered because she was self-conscious about her money.

5. General Motors did not become one of the largest corporations in the United States overnight.

6. This booklet is designed to prevent difficulty for a student who does not know how to study properly.

7. The migrant worker is being exploited, a situation which should be corrected immediately.

8. Senator Taft was a good example of the fact that the conservative position often has great merit.

9. Since it is very noisy, the motor of the car should be repaired as soon as possible.

10. Martin Luther King's dedication to nonviolence influenced him to become a minister.

Exercise 9d

1. We called the fire station near the school when we saw smoke.

2. He had a slight heart attack, but after a month's rest his heart was as good as ever.

3. When he was young he was a good poker player, but now he seldom has time to play.

4. Before we roasted the chicken (duck, goose), we plucked off the feathers.

5. She is a good housekeeper because she learned housekeeping when she was a child.

6. After hearing a lecture on population control, Mrs. Eldon has great respect for the problem.

7. When the witness asked for police protection, four police were assigned to guard him.

8. Although Barbara likes to talk about politics, she does not want to be a politician.

9. A great deal of the fault for children's being irresponsible is that of the parents.

10. My father is a lawyer, but I know nothing about law.

Exercise 9e

1. Central America has revolutions every few months.

2. Throughout the development of the West, the settlers drove back the Indians and took their land.

3. When I called, the CIA said it didn't have any openings for summer jobs.

4. The government pays large sums everywhere except where they are needed.

5. The first few verses of the Bible describe the creation of the world.

6. Every society has to expect that some people will not be able to provide for themselves.

7. The Vietnam agreement said that all American POW's would be released.

8. People in the Victorian era never talked about sex in public.

9. The textbooks say almost nothing about our real treatment of Chicanos and other minorities.

10. Every generation has a "generation gap."

SECTION 10

SHIFTS IN POINT OF VIEW

Shifts in person, number, tense, and mood are errors that students frequently make in their writing. Some shifts, such as those involving a switch of subject or voice in a sentence, are fairly subtle and occasionally occur even in professional writing. You are more likely to be concerned with shifts in person and number. Many students have never been told that shifting from third person to second person, for instance, is incorrect unless done for a compelling reason. Consequently, their papers are littered with general discussions involving "it" and "they" with a few sentences cast in "you should" or "we must" for what students mistakenly think is emphasis. Shifts in person (sometimes more generally referred to simply as shift in point of view) within paragraphs can be just as incongruous as shifts in person within individual sentence.

Exercise 10a-d

1. First clean the surface carefully; then put the glue on. *OR* First the surface should be carefully cleaned; then the glue should be put on.

2. No matter what political party you belong to, you should listen to all the candidates.

3. The Sunday drivers were out in full force, and suddenly there was an accident.

4. He said he had a copy of *Esquire* and asked if I would like to borrow it.

5. I shall be delighted to come if my sister can come with me.

6. South Africa has great supplies of gold while Mexico leads in silver mining.

7. A public opinion poll is based on a cross-section of the population, but sometimes it has been wrong.

8. Mr. Jones put putty around the window panes, and then he repaired the broken sashes.

9. Ruth wondered whether her mother had left and if she had said she would be back.

10. A man needs more than intelligence to be a good legislator; he also has to be a student of human nature.

34

11. The manager decided to offer free samples, and the next day the store was packed with customers.

12. When one feels tired, a candy bar will give him(her) quick energy.

13. He marked the distance from the crosswalk to the curb, and then he painted a heavy yellow line across the area.

14. The college is revising its programs and has asked students to submit suggestions.

15. He asked me if I had done the mathematics problems and if I would lend my paper to him.

MISPLACED PARTS AND DANGLING MODIFIERS

Misplaced parts and dangling modifiers are sentence faults that can promote a great deal of classroom hilarity, since these errors are often of a rather ridiculous nature. For this reason, a little discussion and a few exercises will generally accomplish a great deal because the effects of errors are so often demonstrably ludicrous, hence producing a lasting impression on students. You might begin a discussion of misplaced parts by writing an old classic on the board: "Having been shot in the stern, the captain returned the ship to port." It won't take your class long to discover that here at last is one aspect of English that can be fun.

Subsection 11a of the *Handbook* concerns itself with adverbs such as *almost, hardly,* and *only.* Proper utilization of such adverbs frequently gives students trouble. A good illustrative sentence which brings out very clearly the differences in meaning achieved depending on the placement of the word *only* is the following:

She told Jane to prepare dinner.

Introduction of *only* into the sentence at various places results in the following distinct differences in meaning:

Only she told Jane to prepare dinner.
She *only* told Jane to prepare dinner.
She told *only* Jane to prepare dinner.
She told Jane *only* to prepare dinner.
She told Jane to prepare *only* dinner.
She told Jane to prepare dinner *only*.

The *Handbook* does a nice job of distinguishing between misplaced, squinting, and dangling modifiers: the first has a word in the sentence which it should legitimately modify; the second must try to serve two words and cannot; the third has no word in the sentence with which it can logically be associated. If students will learn the differences among these three types of modification errors, you can save yourself some grading time with shortened explanatory comments, and you can be more specific in the comments you do write.

Exercise 11a

1. He seemed almost amused.

2. The U.S.S. Constitution docked here just last week.

3. The prisoner confessed only when the victim confronted him.

4. Nearly everyone suffers when unemployment rises.

5. Since she had never appeared on a stage before, she was nearly faint from fright.

6. She refused our offer of help merely because she wanted to be independent.

7. Football is sometimes a violent sport, and some players are even badly hurt.

8. The earthquake victims badly needed nurses to bandage their wounds.

9. Reports will be mailed only after the final examinations are finished.

10. The administration provided scarcely any funds for poverty programs.

Exercise 11b

1. Joan borrowed a bicycle with ten speeds from a friend.

2. I kept thinking for the rest of the night how religious my parents were.

3. A small boy in a cowboy suit was found lost on Central Street.

4. After the patrons left the theater, the furnace exploded with a loud crash.

5. For several years, the astronauts looked forward to landing on the moon.

6. He stopped the car on the street before the house with green shutters.

7. In a quivering voice, Susan reported the accident.

8. The President announced at his press conference last week that he would confer with his cabinet.

9. He dropped out of school on Friday after three years' attendance.

10. After he was nearly drowned, the boy was rescued by a lifeguard.

Exercise 11c

1. At Times Square, I took a bus that was going uptown.

2. The new apartment with three bedrooms was in a park.

3. Mary bought from a neighbor a Great Dane that was already housebroken.

4. Shortly after he married, Jones became seriously ill and died.

5. She bought for her husband an alarm clock that was guaranteed for life.

6. He bought from a dealer a sports car that had been completely repainted.

7. After she had graduated from college, she secured a government job which lasted twenty years.

8. Even though it is the most comfortable, we seldom drive this car because the cost is so high.

9. She was knitting for her son a sweater that was warm.

10. On TV we watched the football game that our team won.

Exercise 11d

1. The pilot was told to be prepared constantly for emergencies. *OR* The pilot was told to be prepared for emergencies constantly.

2. After the election, the President said taxes would be cut. *OR* The President said taxes would be cut after the election.

3. The story he was slowly reading put his daughter to sleep. *OR* The story he was reading put his daughter slowly to sleep.

4. The motorcycle he was happily riding skidded off the road.

5. The person who succeeds is intelligent in nine cases out of ten. *OR* In nine cases out of ten, the person who succeeds is intelligent.

6. When the class was over, the instructor told his students they could ask their questions. *OR* The instructor told the class they could ask their questions when the class was over.

7. When it was noon, the passengers were told the plane would take off. *OR* The passengers were told the plane would take off when it was noon.

8. Without doubt, religious faith is a comfort to many people. *OR* Religious faith that knows no doubt is a comfort to many people.

9. The men who were beating on the wall began shooting wildly. *OR* The men who were wildly beating on the wall began shooting.

10. When the movie was over, I promised I would tell her all about it. *OR* I promised I would tell her all about it when the movie was over.

Exercise 11e

1. We agreed once and for all to resolve our partnership.

2. Because the Stephensons quarreled so much, they decided to separate permanently.

3. The problem in South Africa is to persuade successfully the wealthy white rulers to give Blacks a genuine voice in the government.

4. If the weather permits, the team plans to play the game tomorrow.

5. The major nations of the world regularly decide to reduce their armaments one day in the near future.

6. It's helpful to send in your tax return immediately after the first of the year.

7. You have to accept willingly the idea that you are your brother's keeper, or the condition of man will never improve.

8. The owner of the discotheque asked the boys to produce proof of their age immediately.

9. The availability of birth control information helps to reduce effectively the number of unwanted children.

10. The student body voted to abolish fraternities from the campus once and for all.

Exercise 11f

1. Realizing that he was in danger, Abe looked for a way to escape.

2. Emerson, who was a neighbor of Thoreau, lived in a pleasant house in Concord.

3. If you ever see a suspicious prowler, you should immediately call the police.

4. After many years, they discovered the sunken treasure.

5. Despite strong objections from her parents, Peggy is going to study music and painting.

6. After discussing it with his sister, John wrote a letter resigning his position.

7. The Senator's hope was to return to Washington after his long illness.

8. After years of smoking heavily, Swenson made a great effort to stop.

9. For many years Albert Schweitzer lived and worked in a primitive hospital in the jungles of Africa.

10. As many have discovered, pollution is very hard to control.

Exercise 12a

1. He bakes a delicious ham which is cooked in a sweet and sour sauce.

2. As he sat in his cabin, his keen eyes followed the bird's flight.

3. I realized the bridge spanning the Narrows was one of the longest in the world.

4. The airport delays were endless while we waited for the fog to lift.

5. The visitors to wild game preserves must be careful not to excite the fearless and uncaged animals.

6. I could hear the wind howling through the treetops.

7. Since I knew little mathematics, the problem was difficult.

8. When you are seated at an outdoor cafe, Paris reveals an eternal variety.

9. The dog chased me while I was riding my bicycle.

10. While they waited for the coffee to heat, the eggs burned.

Exercise 12b

1. In inspecting the car, he(she) found a large dent in the fender.

2. After the police released the suspect, new evidence was submitted to them.

3. When one decides where to live, he(she) should consider the distance to (his,her) work.

4. In their preparing the launch, they examined the space ship several times.

5. My errors became clear to me when I checked the answer sheet.

6. When one rides in an airplane, the landscape acquires a new beauty.

7. Before he transferred to the new school, his mother took him to meet his future classmates.

8. When I opened the closet door, the boxes on the shelf tumbled down.

9. Because the patient read constantly, the doctor was forced to prescribe glasses.

10. After getting up in the morning, he(she) began the day with a good breakfast.

Exercise 12c

1. To save fuel, turn the thermostat down.

2. To be a good citizen, you must have some knowledge of government procedure.

3. To find out why the wheel shakes, you must drive the car over 50 miles an hour.

4. To plan a college program, you must keep career goals in mind.

5. To be a financial success, a play must have a minimum of 100 performances.

6. If the music is to be appreciated properly, the volume on the record player should be high.

7. If one is to be completely immune to polio, several inoculations may be necessary.

8. For one to become a concert pianist, many years of study are required.

9. Food stamps were issued to eliminate malnutrition among the poor.

10. To make the apartment safe, the lock on the new door was changed.

Exercise 12d

1. Remove the bones when the chicken is well stewed.

2. While I was watching television, someone knocked at the door.

3. If they sighted him, the astronauts would report that the man in the moon really did exist.

4. If it is lost, we shall pay a reward for the ring.

5. If the parents make use of birth control information, the child can arrive exactly when planned.

6. If it is highly polished, you may slip on the floor.

7. My bicycle tire went flat while I was hurrying to the dentist.

8. The car proved hard to drive when I was drinking heavily.

9. If it is well oiled, I find my motorcycle easier to handle.

10. Although the accused was a minor, the judge suspended the sentence.

OMISSIONS; INCOMPLETE AND ILLOGICAL COMPARISONS; AWKWARD OR CONFUSED SENTENCES

Incomplete and illogical comparisons frequently detract from the precision and emphasis of expression. Students will often neglect to indicate <u>what</u> it is that something is *greater than*, as in "We have a greater purpose in life," or will gush that something is "so refreshing" or "so beautiful," all of which hints at a comparison but does not bring it out. Section 13 can help with these problems.

Awkward or confused sentences may result from faulty predication or mixed constructions. As you probably know, if you have graded many compositions, it is far easier to write "AWK" in the margin next to a sentence than it is to explain just why the sentence doesn't "click." Section 14 sheds some light on possible reasons. However, since many of your students will need to worry about far more glaring sentence faults, and since "awkwardness" may mean other things to you, section 14 could reasonable be omitted from class assignment.

The "Basic Sentence Faults" Review Exercise at the end of section 14 is a particularly good one to determine student facility in areas of agreement, reference, and faulty comparisons. If a student can rewrite the exercise sentences well, he or she will have demonstrated a commendable degree of skill in effective sentence composition.

Exercise 13

1. His face is like that of a movie actor.

2. Ghetto children deserve better schools and should be getting them.

3. He made it seem that he wanted to be caught.

4. This quality of mechanism would not be sold in a reputable store.

5. He was both afraid of and fascinated by the idea of skin diving.

6. Midwesterners are as friendly as people in any other section of the country.

7. He made a supreme effort in his senior year and graduated in June.

8. Humphrey was as well known as, if not better known than, any Vice President in history.

9. Which brand of toothpaste reduces cavities?

10. His opinion is in agreement with that of the average individual.

11. She taught in elementary school because she was interested in and capable with young children.

12. I like James Baldwin better than I do any other writer.

13. Adults sometimes understand themselves less well than they do children. *OR* ... less well than children do.

14. He finally decided to give up smoking and eventually wound up doing so.

15. Water colors are much easier than oils.

Exercise 14

1. Harnessing nuclear energy will lessen the needs for other kinds of energy.

2. The copper wheel process provides one of the best types of ornamentation.

3. A traveling salesman has a difficult life, for by the time he gets home he is too tired to talk to or play with his children.

4. Because the government has spent large sums for defense, it has fewer resources to help the poor.

5. Because it is a center for the performing arts, most young actors and actresses yearn to go to New York.

6. He missed the meeting because he forgot the date.

7. Another kind of dishonesty is that involving taxes.

8. My first reaction to being in a large class was one of fright.

9. The car cost me over $3,000.

10. She is leaving because she has been offered a higher salary.

"Basic Sentence Faults" Review Exercise

(Sections 6-14)

1. Harvard generally accepts more students from the Northeast than do other institutions. *OR* Harvard generally accepts more students from the Northeast than it does from other areas. (Basis of comparison is not the same.)

2. After they had been pickled in formaldehyde for a week, the lab instructor distributed the frogs for dissection. (Modifying phrase refers to the wrong subject.)

3. Because Manhattan is an island, you have to take a bridge from New Jersey to reach it. (Phrase is omitted which is essential to sentence meaning.)

4. The boxers having been battered to a pulp, the referee told them the bout was over. (Modifying phrase refers to the wrong subject.)

5. When a teenager begins to lecture to his parents, they feel uncomfortable. (*It* is used in an indefinite manner.)

6. After a year in Vietnam, where he had grown more used to thatched huts, he had forgotten how tall the skyscrapers were. *OR* He had forgotten how tall the skyscrapers were; after a year in Vietnam he had grown more used to thatched huts. (The modifier *after a year* is a squinting modifier.)

7. However much he wanted to get there on time, and with all possible modes of transportation at his disposal, he was destined to fail. (Introductory words *however much* make original construction a sentence fragment.)

8. The letter was mailed an hour ago in the corner mailbox by the new clerk with the red miniskirt. (*In the corner mailbox* is a misplaced modifier.)

9. She likes her better than any of the other girls do. *OR* She likes her better than she does any of the other girls. (Original sentence has an incomplete comparison.)

10. After being graduated from college, Millicent went to work in the theater as a chorus girl. (*After being graduated* is a misplaced modifier.)

MANUSCRIPT MECHANICS

The sections dealing with manuscript mechanics will probably be regarded by many students as the nuisance sections of the book. Manuscript mechanics as such is not an overwhelmingly interesting subject to most writers. Nevertheless, mechanics, even though they may be a very minor aspect of writing, can hardly be regarded as unimportant. After all, unless a manuscript is presented in an attractive format and unless abbreviations are correctly utilized and syllabication is correctly performed, the effect upon the reader can be a distracting one. On the other hand, you will undoubtedly get just as much mileage from these sections by using them for reference rather than assigning them for reading. Students who make numerous mechanics errors in their writing of course should read the relevant sections thoroughly.

It is worth pointing out to your students that little errors have a way of annyoing and infuriating a reader so that he or she ceases to pay attention to the writing's content. Sloppy mechanical errors suggest that if the writer is careless in small matters, he or she may be careless in more important matters as well. Like the individual who spends hours polishing his automobile but who fails to check the oil and water, a careless writer may end up with a thing of beauty that doesn't run very far.

SECTIONS 16-17

NUMBERS AND ABBREVIATIONS

Numbers and abbreviations can be troublesome in composition
writing, and the text provides helpful explanations and exercises.
You may need to note that except in some dates "1st," "2nd," "3rd,"
etc. are not acceptable substitutes for "first," "second," and
"third" in formal writing. Also, students frequently need to be
reminded that they must spell out numbers less than one hundred and
that they should do so consistently. The "Manuscript" Review Exercise at the end of section 18 makes a good diagnostic quiz as well
as a check to see if your class has become sufficiently familiar
with mechanics.

Exercise 16

1. John Kennedy was inaugurated January 20, 1961, at the age of
   forty-four.

2. The students' strike lasted ten days.

3. The satellite model measured 5.19 inches in circumference.

4. Steven spent two years in the Peace Corps.

5. The seminar met at 2:30 P.M.

6. Some people spend as much as ninety-five cents for bus fare
   daily.

7. Eighty-five thousand people viewed the President's press conference.

8. Labor Day is the first Monday in September.

9. Retail prices were found to be nearly 15 percent higher in the
   ghetto than in other areas of the city.

10. Of 500 students in the senior class, only 150 attended
    the prom. *OR* Of five hundred students in the senior
    class, only one hundred fifty attended the prom.

Exercise 17

1. At 2 P.M., the rocket was launched.

2. The President and Ambassador Smith discussed United States
   policy in the South Pacific.

3. He enrolled in the University of Maine because he liked
   the New England climate.

46

4. Mr. Turner spent his August vacation working with a civil rights group in Alabama.

5. Mr. Downs noted the license number of the motorcycle.

6. After years of study in chemistry, he decided to become a doctor.

7. Many mountain passes are closed in the winter in Switzerland.

8. The English professor asked the students to draw on their personal experiences in writing compositions.

9. The urban renewal project will cover the area from Main Street to Michigan Avenue.

10. Next fall the university will offer courses in Black Literature and Black History.

11. The doctor told his patient to take three teaspoonsful of medicine every two hours.

12. The shortest day of the year is in December.

13. Reverend Paul Crocker's sermons draw upon his training in philosophy.

14. The roads are impassable because of a flood this morning.

15. The Captain spent all his dollars on his October furlough.

SECTION 18

SYLLABICATION

Now and again you will discover a student who has never heard that words broken at the ends of lines must be divided between syllables. Most people divide words "by ear," and nine times out of ten they do so correctly. However, mispronunciation and regional pronunciation can lead to faulty syllabication. Dictionary consultation is the only sure guide. Consequently, you may want to emphasize the use of the dictionary or a spelling word list as an effective aid to proper syllabication, as well as the helpful rules which are cited in the text. Spelling word lists and "word books" have been marketed by many publishers and are generally obtainable at a very low price. Such a list or book can be one of a student's most helpful possessions because it can provide quick assistance in matters of spelling and syllabication.

Exercise 18

drowned	twelve	au-to-mo-bile
swim-mer	through	ex-er-cise
learn-ed	(Only if used as an adjective: a *learned* man.)	
abrupt	acute	open
en-ve-lope	ex-president	pre-eminent
enough	walked	

"Manuscript" Review Exercise

(Sections 15-18)

1. Some stores put a service charge on bills that are not paid within thirty days.

2. I try not to enroll in classes that begin before 10:45 A.M.

3. The vice president of the student coucil is occasionally asked to act as chairman of the meetings.

4. The new center for African Studies will be located at Maple and Main Streets.

5. Three boxtops must accompany every request for a "free" sample.

6. Paperback books, which once sold for a quarter, now cost as much as $5.95.

7. The local movie house will show a Bogart film on the first Monday of every month.

8. Most tourists in New York go to see the Empire State Building first.

9. Some people opposed extending suffrage to eighteen-year-olds.

10. Students should have a voice in such things as curriculum development and course selection.

11. The Moore Manufacturing Company gave all old customers a 5 percent reduction on snow tires.

12. All heavyweight boxers must be over 175 pounds.

13. All perch measuring under five inches must be thrown back into Lake Mendota.

14. Reverend Winters performed the marriage ceremony at the Lutheran Church.

15. Mr. and Mrs. Hone entered their three-year-old filly in the race.

PUNCTUATION

During your career as a composition teacher, you will probably expend more red ink on faulty punctuation than on any other writing error. Many students assume punctuation comes naturally, like breathing, to be dropped into sentences where it "feels right." But if they breathe like they punctuate, some must turn blue from lack of periods and others suffer hiccups from a surfeit of commas. Far from being unimportant, punctuation can be essential to interpreting the meaning of a sentence.

Proper placement of commas, for example, tells a reader precisely what emphasis the writer wishes for certain clauses and phrases. Punctuation groups, divides, and arranges thoughts and portions of thoughts into meaningful and coherent communicative messages. Lack of proper punctuation may at times not make a vital difference; at other times it may destroy accuracy and precision, detracting greatly from effective expression.

When we speak we have volume, pacing, rhythm, inflection of pitch and tone, and body language to help us make meanings clear. When we write our resources are more limited: along with word choice and sentence structure, effective punctuation is one of the few available tools.

The *Handbook* considers the problem of proper punctuation from the perspective of four different functions: end punctuation, internal punctuation, direct quotation punctuation, and word punctuation. A number of exercises are provided both within and at the end of sections relating to each of these functions. In addition, a "punctuation" review exercise covers all the aspects of punctuation treated in sections 19-30. The latter exercise can be used as an excellent test of students' comprehensive understanding of correct punctuation.

SECTION 19

END PUNCTUATION

End punctuation usually does not give students much difficulty, although some have trouble distinguishing between a statement which asks a direct question and a statement which contains an
indirect question. The use of periods with abbreviations is also
sometimes an area of concern; and, although the text does give
examples of proper usage, it will often be necessary to stress, as
does the text, that a good dictionary must be consulted wherever
there is doubt whether an abbreviation should be used.

Ellipsis may be a wholly unknown form of punctuation for some
students. Although they have surely seen ellipsis in print, students may not be sure why or how it should be used. If they are
writing compositions containing quotations from other sources, a
knowledge of ellipses can be very handy.

Exercise 19(1)

1. The reporter asked, "Mr. President, could you clarify that
   remark please?"

2. "Yes," he replied, "let me make that absolutely clear."

3. Mr. C. P. Johnson, who formerly worked with the law firm of
   Herrick, Noble, and Snow, is now with the U. S. Army.

4. Periods used in or omitted from some abbreviations often
   depend on the custom of the organization or institution
   itself. For example, *UCLA* and *MIT* are customarily
   written without periods.

5. New York City is customarily written out fully or
   abbreviated *NYC*, without periods.

6. Recently we have learned much about the F.B.I. and the
   C.I.A. *OR* the FBI and the CIA

7. Is Mrs. or Miss the abbreviation for Mistress?

8. "May I quote you on that, Mr. President?" asked the reporter.

9. "Oh, why do you insist on quoting everything?" he cried.

10. The guard yelled, "Halt!"

Exercise 19(2)

I remember that . . . I used to see Tarzan movies on Satur-
day. White Tarzan used to beat up the black natives. I would
sit there yelling, "Kill the beasts . . . ." I was saying:
Kill me. It was as if a Jewish boy watched Nazis taking Jews
off to concentration camps and cheered them on. Today, I
want the chief to beat hell out of Tarzan and send him back
to Europe . . . .

51

SECTION 20

INTERNAL PUNCTUATION: MAIN CLAUSES

A word about commas: it seems a relatively simple thing to remember to put commas before coordinating conjunctions linking two independent clauses. Nevertheless, many students have to be reminded repeatedly. Even more problematic is the habit of inserting a comma before every coordinating conjunction, whether it occurs between independent clauses or not: for example, "The car crashed into the barrier, and burst into flames." If your students suffer from this "knee-jerk" comma reaction at the sight of a coordinating conjunction, it is likely that they really have not learned to distinguish between compound sentences and compound elements (such as subjects, predicates, etc.) within sentences. A review of sentence structure is in order.

Semicolons have previously been discussed to some extent in section 7 of this manual. Actually, the semicolon has only two basic purposes: separation of independent sentence elements and separation of items in series containing their own internal punctuation. Again, you may find that problems arise not from a misunderstanding of the use of the semicolon but from an inability to recognize independent and dependent sentence elements. Consequently, exercises in the use of the semicolon may indicate a need for additional student work in basic sentence structure--in other words, the trouble may be basically a grammatical one rather than a mechanical one.

The colon is another punctuation mark which can add versatility to a student's writing. In many instances the colon can be used interchangeably with the semicolon; however, where the second main clause does not amplify or explain the first, the semicolon is required and not the colon. This distinction is difficult for students to grasp, and, indeed, sometimes you will be hard pressed to distinguish the difference yourself. Wide reading and familiarity with the way others have used the semicolon and colon are more effective teachers than any explanation or exercise. Correct usage comes with a feeling for language and context--something, unfortunately, few students possess.

One way to sharpen the distinction between the colon and semicolon is to emphasize that in the case of the semicolon, except where items in series with internal punctuation are involved, those sentence elements which come before and after the semicolon must be independent in structure. By comparison, where a colon is required, what comes before the colon must be an independent element but what comes after it does not have to be.

Sentences dealing with the same subject matter can be worded so as to require either the semicolon or the colon.

52

He liked all kinds of vegetables; he particularly liked peas, beans, collards, and potatoes.

He liked all kinds of vegetables: peas, beans, collards, and potatoes.

In the first of the above sentences, a colon could be substituted for the semicolon and the sentence sense would remain the same. In the second sentence, though, the semicolon could not be substituted for the colon, since what comes after the colon is only a list of items and not an independent clause.

Exercise 20(1)

1. The telephone call brought them news they had been waiting for: Doris had been offered a position with IBM.

2. One of Will Rogers' assets was his grin; seldom is such a grin seen except on an Oklahoman.

3. The cat tried to catch the goldfish, but in his excitement he fell into the bowl.

4. Very few of the workers had been able to get to the office the morning of the blizzard; the manager decided to close the office.

5. Good intentions are not enough: intelligence is needed also.

6. One record was lost and two were broken, but the rest arrived safely.

7. Many students are ambitious to become lawyers; however, few realize the amount of work necessary.

8. Crime rates have been increasing rapidly; therefore, demands for stricter law enforcement increase rapidly.

9. Many scientists believe that marijuana is no more harmful than alcohol; nevertheless, alcohol is legal but marijuana is not.

10. Every winter the fear of energy shortages is renewed; every summer the fear is forgotten.

Exercise 20(2)

1. Public opinion polls indicated that Mrs. Kennedy's popularity had declined after her marriage to Onassis; still, it was not clear whether this was the sole reason.

2. European housewives shop daily; consequently, they do not have left-over food to throw away.

3. Student demonstrations were becoming increasingly violent; school administrators adopted a "get tough" attitude.

4. There were some congested areas on the highway; still, for the most part, traffic flowed smoothly.

5. The witness was positive that these were the men--they had rushed into the bank in broad daylight and held the employees at gunpoint.

6. Strong efforts must be made to bridge the gap between the races, or this nation will be split into two separate societies.

7. Common sense is not a very common quality; therefore, those who possess it are usually sought after.

8. At that time, the Smiths thought nothing of the occasional signs of oil on the floor of the garage although they recalled later that their oil tank needed constant refilling.

9. The thundershower ended as quickly as it had begun, the spectators filed back into their seats, and the baseball game was resumed.

10. The reports waited patiently for the President until noon; then they began to batter the press secretary with questions.

SECTION 21

SUBORDINATE PHRASES AND CLAUSES

Students may find it easier to remember the comma after an introductory phrase or subordinate clause if you tell them to think of the comma as a flag--a signal to readers that the main clause is about to begin. Also, if they remember that conjunctive adverbs and verbals, in many cases, indicate subordinate clauses, they should be prepared to insert a comma in mid-sentence when they see these words at the head of sentence.

Troubles may arise, though, where types of expressions that often precede main clauses are inserted after the main clauses. In such instances, in addition to the instructions set forth in section 21c, the voice itself can often be used as a guide to determine whether or not punctuation is required. Note in the following sentences how the voice inflection either does or does not indicate emphasis.

There is nothing to worry about unless it rains (no real concern on the part of the speaker that it will rain).

There is nothing to worry about, unless it rains (a sense of foreboding on the part of the speaker that it will rain).

Exercise 21(1)

1. After visiting several hospitals, she became interested in a career in physical therapy.

2. Because of the high risk of injury, motorcycle riders in most states are required to wear helmets.

3. To one who is interested in farming, land has beauty and character.

4. Having finished a course in photography, she began taking pictures of all her friends.

5. As we expected, prices continued to rise throughout the year.

6. After he had signed, the contract was placed in the safe.

7. No comma required.

8. After he had finished his journalism courses, he worked as a part-time reporter for the *Wakefield Times*.

9. In spite of their good intentions, most parents don't understand their children.

10. Forced to make an emergency landing, the pilot let the plane lose altitude rapidly.

1. During his final exile on the island of St. Helena, Napoleon may have been poisoned. (Comma is needed after introductory prepositional phrase.)

2. Having turned state's evidence, Crawford was given a lighter sentence. (Comma is needed after introductory participial phrase.)

3. When the exam was placed in front of him, he realized how little he had studied. (Comma is needed after introductory adverbial clause.)

4. With the shift of Daylight Time in spring, everyone loses an hour's sleep. (Comma is needed after introductory prepositional phrase.)

5. If dry weather continues through the spring, wheat crops will suffer greatly. (Comma is needed after introductory subordinate clause.)

6. Shortly before, the committee meeting ended. (Comma is needed after the introductory adverbs to achieve correct sentence emphasis and meaning.)

7. Comma after *Thanksgiving* is optional. The meaning will be clear with or without it.

8. Sentence is correct as given.

9. Annoyed by the coughing of the audience, John Barrymore once stalked off the stage during a performance. (Comma is needed after the introductory participial phrase.)

10. Sentence is correct as given.

NONRESTRICTIVES AND OTHER PARENTHETICAL ELEMENTS;
ITEMS IN A SERIES: FINAL APPOSITIVES AND SUMMARIES

Restrictive and nonrestrictive sentence elements can be a no man's land of confusion for both instructor and students. Especially when discussing the exercises, you and your class may find yourselves locking horns over whether an expression is restrictive or not. However, placing commas after the fact in these types of sentences may be to approach the problem from the wrong end. Stress to your students that the use of commas is <u>their</u> way of telling a reader how <u>they</u> intend modifying information to be understood.

Nonrestrictive modifiers add nonessential amplifying information and require commas to show their parenthetical nature. Restrictive elements are integral to a sentence's meaning and need no commas. But rather than always puzzling this out mentally, students may best discover whether expressions are restrictive or nonrestrictive by applying a voice test. Tell them to say the sentence in question aloud. The voice will invariably drop before and after a nonrestrictive expression but will not do so where a restrictive expression is involved.

Modifiers will <u>become</u> either restrictive or nonrestrictive according to whether commas are or are not used. Sentences such as the following can help to prove this point.

> Probationary students who fail their courses
> will have to repeat some classes.
>
> Probationary students, who fail their courses,
> will have to repeat some classes.
>
> Little children who don't like vegetables need
> vitamin supplements.
>
> Little children, who don't like vegetables,
> need vitamin supplements.

The dash is another very useful mark of punctuation. However, once some students learn that a dash can be used for dramatic emphasis, their flair for the dramatic may result in dash-studded writing. Consequently, you may have to emphasize repeatedly the judicious use of dashes, restricting them mainly to short final appositives. On the other hand, the contrasting emphasis obtained by the substitution of the dash for parenthesis, or vice versa, may be appropriate, as is illustrated by the sentences below.

Joe Doakes (the best football player in the
conference) was a straight A student.

Joe Doakes--the best football player in the
conference--was a straight A student.

Exercise 22(1)

1. John L. Lewis, an aggressive union leader, was self-educated.

2. No one, not even his wife, knows what Tony paid for his collection of jazz records.

3. Sentence is correct as given. *who know what they are talking
about* is a restrictive clause. *OR* Commuters, *who know what
they are talking about,* complain bitterly over the state of
public transportation. (The *who* clause can be construed as
nonrestrictive: commuters as a general class contrasted to
non-commuters.)

4. Students who do not wish medical insurance should turn in
blank cards; the others, who are evidently satisfied with the
insurance, should fill in all details.

5. Sentence is correct as given. *and best* is a restrictive modifier.

6. Enrico Fermi, who has been called the architect of the atomic
age, was born in Italy.

7. The siege of Troy, which is the subject of the *Iliad*, lasted
for ten years.

8. Sentence is correct as given.

9. His attempt to win her back was, as you can guess, unsuccessful.

10. Julian Bond, although still a young man, is being watched with
interest by older politicians.

Exercise 22(2)

1. Mr. Wright, who is the town's oldest citizen, walks to work
daily.

2. Sentence is correct as given.

3. Binghampton, the largest city in the area, was hard hit by
floods.

4. Sentence is correct as given. *which hibernate in the winter*
is restrictive.

5. The owner of the Green Dragon, having been convicted of negli-
gence, was fined $1,000.

6. Heart transplants, once confined to science fiction, are now
standard medical practice.

7. Sentence is correct as given.

8. Sentence is correct as given. (*that my mother prefers* is restrictive.)

9. Traveling in Asia, if one is willing to experiment with new foods, can be exciting.

10. On Christmas, which came on Friday last year, there was a record-breaking storm.

Exercise 23

1. The warehouse had an aluminum roof, a concrete floor, and a steel windowsash.

2. His courses included algebra, which he liked; psychology, which he at least found interesting; and French, which he hated.

3. Both candidates seemed to be promising peace, prosperity, and happiness.

4. He learned how necessary money is, how hard it is to earn, and how easy it is to spend.

5. He brought a pot of strong, steaming hot coffee to the table.

6. Among the countries I visited last summer were Rumania, Bulgaria, and Poland--all behind the Iron Curtain.

7. The telephone operator reported that there was no 33 Pine Drive in Austin, that there is no Michael Stone listed at any other address, and that there is no telephone exchange beginning with 254 in that area.

8. To pursue a career in the theater, one must have talent, a great deal of energy, and a supreme confidence in himself.

9. If TV commercials are to be believed, the American dream consists of a new car, a color television set, and a mate who uses an effective mouthwash.

10. Taking off his wrinkled old white cap, lowering his tattered black umbrella, and scraping his tennis shoes on the doormat, he rang the bell.

Exercise 24

1. She was a good teacher--good humored, clever, always clear.

2. He had absolutely no virtues at all; he would lie, cheat, or steal at every opportunity.

3. These are the punctuation marks that give the most difficulty: commas, semicolons, and colons.

4. He had only one pleasure--eating.

5. His whole life seems devoted to one activity--football.

6. Four complex civilizations existed in America many years before the white man arrived: the Olmec, the Toltec, the Aztec, and the Mayan.

7. Everything for the trip will be ready: the car checked, the baggage loaded, the money in hand.

8. He sometimes seems to care about only one thing--his dog Ruffles.

9. To learn to play the piano well, you need three things: a good teacher, a great deal of patience, and several thousand hours of practice.

10. The short story was only a pot boiler--estimated life one month.

SECTION 25

SUPERFLUOUS INTERNAL PUNCTUATION

Sometimes, one of the most difficult student punctuation errors to correct is overpunctuation. Many students seem to have a compulsive tendency to automatically insert commas in sentences where commas are definitely out of place. This type of student will frequently write sentences such as the following:

My car is, for sale.

She hit the ball, a long distance.

An engineering student, enrolled in my art class.

He disliked, every moment of his army career.

The ball, of blue yarn, unraveled, slowly.

The tendency to inject commas between subjects and verbs, verbs and complements, verbs and objects and integral units of sentences may be indicative only of a lack of knowledge of proper punctuation; it may, on the other hand, be indicative of a lack of knowledge of effective sentence structure. You may clarify the situation somewhat if you point out to your class the many kinds of modifiers, such as ordinary prepositional phrases and single adverbs or adjectives, do not require commas to set them off from the words they modify.

Exercise 25

1. Across the river was a protected cove in which there were two rowboats and one small sailboat.

2. The meeting began late because Blackburn did not know where the Regency Motel was or when the meeting was scheduled.

3. The pilot having received clearances, the plane circled the field before landing.

4. Robbins decided he could not take the night job and still take courses in chemistry, accounting, and history in the mornings.

5. The ice near the southern bank was too thin and soft to support the child's weight.

6. Nobody knows what the men who work under the Secretary of State really think of him or of his policies.

7. Nudity on the public stage, once undreamed of but now common-ly accepted, may eventually run out its course and be re-ceived only with apathy.

8. The senator replied slowly because he had not expected the question, and he really didn't know what to say.

9. Sentence is correct as given.

10. The disenchantment with urban renewal stems from the fact that frequently it is merely a matter of building new slums to replace the old.

"Internal Punctuation" Review Exercises

(Sections 20-25)

1. Outside, the dog scratched on the door.

2. Judy went shopping, Marty went to a movie, and Lou stayed home to nurse her cold.

3. Answering the defense, attorney Robbins said angrily he was sure of his evidence. *OR* Answering the defense attorney, Robbins said angrily he was sure of his evidence.

4. Uranium, which is important in atomic processes, is found in parts of Africa.

5. The Governor refused, to everyone's surprise and bewilder-ment, to sign the bill after the Senate passed it.

6. Mark, our plumber who can bend iron pipe in his bare hands, recited Shakespeare as he fixed our water pipes.

7. Words, words, words were all that came out of the meeting.

8. Common sense is not a common quality: those who have it are often sought after.

9. The President, critics say, has gained too much power in foreign affairs at the expense of the Senate.

10. A quiet stretch of Sudbury farmland, set behind a row of tidy, typical colonials, is the setting of the story.

11. Mr. Goldberg, who was once U. S. Ambassador to the U. N., was also once an Associate Justice of the Supreme Court.

12. There's only one problem involved in "doing your own thing"--that's that everyone else may want to do his own thing as well.

13. It's relatively easy to borrow money--it's much harder to pay it back.

14. Jealousy, a debilitating emotion, can wreck a relationship, for without genuine trust there can be no real love.

15. There is some evidence to show that Christopher Columbus was not the first European to visit America; recent discoveries reveal that there may have been Viking settlements on the northeastern tip of the continent.

SECTION 26

PUNCTUATION OF QUOTED MATERIAL

The punctuation of quoted material sometimes causes difficulty for students who cannot distinguish between a direct and an
indirect quotation. If you have students with this problem, you
may want to assign additional work such as exercises from the
Prentice-Hall Workbook for Writers. Quotations within quotations,
how to refer to a word used in a special sense, and how to punctuate long quotations may also need special emphasis.

Probably the most frequently violated quotation punctuation
rule is that regarding punctuation at the end of quotations.
Students cannot seem to remember that <u>all</u> periods and commas should
be placed <u>inside</u> the quotation marks, regardless of their relationship to the quoted material. If you have discovered an effective
way to etch this in your students' memories, let us know about it!

Exercise 26

1. The letter said tartly, "The fault is not with our product
    but with your skin; it appears to be supersensitive."

2. "Perhaps you might like to do a study of the sexual imagery
    in Shakespeare," the professor suggested.

3. "How long have you noticed this condition?" the doctor asked.

4. As the history professor said in his class yesterday, "There
    is no real evidence that Marie Antoinette ever said 'Let them
    eat cake!'"

5. He said, "When the policeman asked me 'Where's the fire?' I
    felt like giving him an equally sarcastic answer."

6. The song "Aquarius" is from the musical *Hair*.

7. Arthur Schlesinger, Jr. says John Stuart Mill wrote a century
    ago, "The greatness of England is now all collective; individ-
    ually small, we appear capable of anything great only by our
    habit of combining."

8. The salesclerk said, "Sir, I would exchange this sweater,
    but," he added, "it has already been worn."

9. One day, just as I was going out to Rahul's house, I heard
    her shouting outside the door of the study. "The director is
    a busy man!"she was shouting. She had her back against the
    door and held her arms stretched out; M. stood in front of
    her and his head was lowered. "Day after day you come and
    eat his life up!" she said.

10. I climbed up in the bar yelling "Walsh, I'm shot! I'm shot!" I could feel the blood running down my leg. Walsh, the fellow who operated the fish-and-chips joint, pushed me off the bar and onto the floor. I couldn't move now, but I was still completely conscious. Walsh was saying, "Git outta here, kid. I ain't got no time to play." A woman was screaming, mumbling something about the Lord, and saying, "Somebody done shot that poor child."

ITALICS; CAPITALS; APOSTROPHE; HYPHEN

Word punctuation involving italics, capitalization, and possession is admittedly a minor aspect of writing; yet, mistakes in word punctuation detract from the overall quality of writing and give the impression that the writer is very careless or un-sophisticated. In this connection, you might mention to your class that use of the word "it's" as the possessive of "it" is probably one of the four or five most misspelled words in the English lan-guage. Similarly, "their," which is supposed to indicate the pos-sessive of "they," is a very widely misspelled word. Of course, what is really involved here is most probably not misspelling at all but a lack of understanding of how to form the possessive of these words. Again, an understanding of basic structure and func-tion can prevent these embarrassing errors in writing.

Exercise 27

1. James Earl Jones, the eminent black actor, received a Tony award for his broadway performance in *The Great White Hope*.

2. *H.M.S. Queen Elizabeth*, for years the flagship of the Cunard Line, was finally retired from service.

3. Are you supposed to pronounce the *p* in *coup de grâce*?

4. Some Americans use the word *simpatico* as though it meant *sympathetic*, but its meaning is closer to that of the English word *charming*.

5. Is T. S. Eliot's *The Wasteland* included in *The Oxford Book of English Verse*?

6. His travels had brought him greater understanding of himself and just a touch of *savoir-faire*.

7. *Webster's Third New International Dictionary* lists more than half a dozen pronunciations of *lingerie*.

8. I am constantly forgetting what *eclectic* means.

9. New Englanders tend to add an *r* to words that end in an *a* and to omit the *r* in words that do end in *r*.

10. Thus, in Boston, *Cuba* becomes *Cuber*, while *river* becomes *riva*.

Exercise 28

1. After leaving Detroit, we turned north toward Mackinac Island for our summer vacation with Uncle Jim.

2. The Reverend Martin Luther King, Jr. first came to public attention as a leader of the civil rights sit-ins in the South.

3. The late Robert Kennedy had been Attorney General of the United States before being elected senator from the state of New York.

4. It has been predicted that power in the UN will shift from the Security Council to the General Assembly.

5. The Boston Symphony Orchestra is not to be confused with the Boston Pops Orchestra.

6. All math majors who were preparing to teach elementary school students were required by the math department to take courses in the new math.

7. The Organization of American States is designed to encourage cooperation and understanding among the nations of the Western Hemisphere.

8. Michael O'Hara, president of the student congress, addressed the meeting.

9. Many of the Aberdeen Angus cattle come from the state of Nebraska.

10. It was the fall of the Roman Empire which ushered in the Middle Ages.

Exercise 29

1. One of my most prized possessions is the Supremes' first record album.

2. It's hard to believe that in a country as rich as ours, some people still go to bed hungry every night.

3. The Chairman's secretary has assured all members of the department that they'll have their class schedules in two weeks' time.

4. Most modern cities haven't the resources with which to keep up with their expanding population.

5. He had asked for a month's leave of absence, but he was allowed to take only the three days' sick leave that were due him.

6. Sentence is correct as given.

7. What's the point of experimenting with mind-expanding drugs when they can do terrible damage to one's mind?

8. A rock group's career, as show business goes, is relatively short.

9. The greatest years of *The New Yorker* were those under Harold Ross's editorship.

67

10. It's hard to keep up with the Joneses when you don't have Mr. Jones's income.

Exercise 30

1. The editor-in-chief owns a well-designed house.

2. He boasts that he is self-made and self-educated, but he forgets that he is also self-centered.

3. My father-in-law once ran in the hundred-meter relay; his team went as far as the semifinals.

4. The lifelong dream of many Americans is a four-bedroom home with a two-car garage.

5. He changed a twenty-dollar bill into five-dollar bills.

Review Exercise 27-30

1. Magazines such as *Yankee* and *Vermont Life* are popular with readers who idolize old-time country life.

2. The item appeared in last Monday's *New York Times*.

3. It's a well-known fact that most old-age pensions are inadequate for present-day needs.

4. Sarah's ex-husband had been well-meaning enough but too self-effacing for an outgoing girl's taste.

5. He's got too many *ands* in his sentences.

6. Barbra Streisand's first big break in show business was in the Broadway play, *I Can Get It for You Wholesale.*

7. The four American delegates' carefully prepared proposal was rejected by the Soviet Union's spokesman.

8. Although eighteen-year-olds can now vote, my brother's friend didn't vote until he was twenty-one.

9. The four-cylinder, sixty-horsepower car wasn't able to pull Jones's custom-buit limousine out of the ditch.

10. *Roots,* an eight-pa t dramatic series based on Alex Haley's search for his long-buried past, topped all previous TV programs in the Nielsen ratings.

"Punctuation" Review Exercises

(Sections 19-30)

Exercise A

1. Her favorite writers--Joyce Carol Oates and James Dickey--are both contemporary.

2. His faults are an uncontrollable temper, inexperience, and indifference to his work.

3. Since we had driven the car 87,000 miles, we decided to turn it in.

4. If *siege* is spelled with an *ie*, why is *seize* spelled with an *ei*?

5. "What we need," said Mr. Blevin, the union spokesman, "is a good day's pay for a good day's work."

6. Many people, perhaps most people, do not know from what materials their cereals, plastics, and clothing are made.

7. The government was faced with a difficult task: it had to persuade a skeptical, frustrated people that the energy shortage was real.

8. Her camera, her new dress, and her books, all of which she had left in her car, had been stolen.

9. I have just received an unexpected letter from the Director of the Bureau of Internal Revenue.

10. Ruth wanted a Pontiac; Francis, a Ford; Donna, a Chrysler; and Alice, a Raleigh bicycle.

11. The late Will Rogers's favorite saying was, "I've never met a man I didn't like."

12. Judy Garland is best remembered for her role in the 1930's film, *The Wizard of Oz*.

13. Does anyone remember who said, "Absolute power corrupts absolutely"?

14. I make it a point to read the *New York Times* every day and the *New Yorker* every week; only rarely, however, do I get around to *Time* or *Newsweek*.

15. "You can't do that!" she cried hysterically, "You can't! You can't!"

Exercise B

"Trip" describes the psychedelic experience very well. "It is gratuitous, an extra day in the week," one saying goes, and the sense of this experience being unearned is perhaps the common feature of all the attitudes that have grown up around it. It shapes the disbelief of those who have not experienced it; and, paradoxically, it confirms the belief that something quite so rich in life experience must somehow always be a gift and unmerited. The view of ordinary life is nearly always altered after a trip, but this does not mean the style of post-psychedelic life is set or naturally follows. Egos are still distinct twins in their variety; and the egoless, the genuine LSD head, can't really be said to have returned from his trip. You can't bring the universe home with you; perhaps all you can do is choose your home.

Exercise C

1. I've seen the play *Hello Dolly* twice, but I still find its plot fascinating. (*It's* is not the possessive of *it* but the contraction of *it is*.)

2. We like to think that the spoils system went out with Andrew Jackson, but actually it's still in effect in federal, state, and municipal government. (There should be no colon after *effect*.)

3. Isn't it time we all ignored our own personal problems and cooperated with one another in making this world a better place to live in? (Apostrophe comes after *n* in *isn't*. The sentences is a question and must end with a question mark.)

4. She watches television all day long and in the evening too. (A semicolon is used to separate independent sentence elements. *and in the evening too* is not independent.)

5. Should one judge a candidate from the speeches he makes? From the printed matter he distributes? Or, from the ideas he generates? (A question mark as an end-stop of punctuation is required here after the constructions phrased as questions. Alternatively, the prepositional phrases could be separated with commas and the question mark placed only at the end.)

6. This sentence is correctly punctuated.

7. The President's daughters' (daughter's) activities are always reported in the press; so are his wife's. (Apostrophes to denote possession are required for *President, daughter,* and *wife.* A semicolon is needed after *press* to separate independent clauses.)

8. I think I recognize that actor--wasn't he on the television show *My Three Sons?* (A dash here best indicates the turn in direction of thought.)

9. "I wanted to make that perfectly clear," the President said. "Have I made it so?" (The sentences are a split direct quotation.)

10. As one pundit once observed of Senator Humphrey, "He couldn't be accused of using any greasy kid stuff!" (A direct quotation is involved. The sentence could be written without the exclamation point, depending upon the assumption that is made concerning the speaker's tone of voice.)

LARGER ELEMENTS

Sections 31-32 cover the bulk of material students will need
for the composition writing process. These sections begin by considering topic choosing and end with paragraph writing. Naturally,
if you prefer to begin with paragraphs and conclude with the whole
composition, you can change the order in which you assign the individual units.

One of the most difficult aspects of composition writing is
subject matter--or topic choosing. Many students, left to their
own devices, will take the position that there is really nothing
they want to write about or nothing to write about that they want
to devote much attention to. Obviously, if a means can be found
to interest them in a subject, the chances of their writing effectively will be enhanced considerably. In this connection, since a
list of suggested subjects will often be helpful, paragraph 31a
with its accompanying exercises may assist the student in exploring
specific facets of a broad general subject.

Another method that many instructors have used successfully is
to require students to write compositions based on reading assignments. This method can provide subject matter for which the student is held responsible and will often accomplish the additional
objective of furthering his knowledge in a specific area. In other
instances, reading material can provoke interest in matters of
student concern and motivate individual responses to issues which
have been raised.

But even when reading material is assigned, some students may
find it difficult to do much more than write a summary of what they
have read. In cases like these, the reading is dictating to the
students rather than stimulating them. One way you can loosen this
mental log jam is to practice some thinking "out loud" on the blackboard with the class. Pick a couple of provocative paragraphs from
the reading material and ask your students to propose as many topics
as they can that are even remotely suggested by the paragraph material. Write these on the board as phrases which indicate the direction compositions on these subjects might take; even better, ask
the students to phrase the topics when they suggest them. The
point here, obviously, is not necessarily to stick to the main line
of development in the reading material itself but to "spin off"
ideas quickly--to "pull out the stops." You will have to ask yourself if your primary goal is to have the class analyze reading
material in their compositions or simply to have them write acceptable essays. Many instructors have found that if they insist on
the analysis-type composition too early in a writing course, students will suffer from "can't think of anything to say" because
they are not yet comfortable enough with writing to handle the
more sophisticated requirements of analysis. The results will
probably be more satisfactory to everyone if you allow a great
deal of freedom in topic choice on the earlier compositions at

least. Reading material can be used for class discussion and to
get the ball rolling on possible topics.

After you have constructed a list of ten or twelve topics on
the board, ask students to pick the four they find most interesting. Erase all the others, and concentrate on these four--one at
a time--having the class narrow each topic to manageable size,
propose a thesis statement, and roughly outline an essay using
that thesis as the starting point. You can participate as much as
is necessary to keep the discussion moving. Experiencing a "dry
run" of this type usually gives a class the confidence it needs to
handle topic choosing and preliminary thinking on its own. Collective brainstorming can make the process look a lot less forbidding. The following lists show how one class used a magazine article on fast food restaurants to develop manageable and interesting
essay topics.

General Subject—Fast Food Restaurants

Possible Topics

> history of fast food in America
> types of fast food restaurants
> cost of a fast food meal vs a home-cooked meal
> * locations of fast food restaurants
> fashions of fast food staff uniforms
> nutritional value of fast food meals
> curb-service: what happened to it?
> working in a fast food restaurant
> ** why fast food restaurants are popular

*Thesis Paragraph**

> The dependence of the average American upon the automobile
> is a key to the location of most fast food restaurants.
> The nearest Macdonald's is not a substitute for the corner
> cafe or the neighborhood soda fountain of fifty years ago.
> You can't just drop in to a Burger Chef after a leisurely
> evening stroll around your block. No, fast food stores are
> a phenomenon of the freeway, the shopping center, the
> business loop, and modern suburban sprawl.

*Thesis Paragraph***

> Fast food restaurants are popular among Americans because
> they suit our lifestyle. We like consistency, economy,
> and speed with our meals. We like a clean, no-frills,
> casual atmosphere in which to eat. And most important of
> all, we like HAMBURGERS!

Writing in generalities is an occupational hazard of student
composition writing. The emphasis here, consequently, must be on
saying a lot about a little rather than a little about a lot. The
key is a very thorough knowledge of the prospective subject. A
person who really understands the subject of football, for example,
will be able to say a great deal about the types of blocks that an
offensive tackle will be required to make--on such a subject, he
can go into very great detail upon one narrow phase of the game,

72

and this is exactly the sort of thing that is generally desired in
a conventional length freshman composition. Similarly, returning
to the fast food topics, one student who had spent his summer vacation as a "pickle slinger" at a drive-in restaurant wrote a detailed description of hamburger preparation which he titled "...on a
Sesame Seed Bun."

SECTION 31

THE WHOLE COMPOSITION

After topic selection, many instructors feel the most important aspect of composition writing is formulating a thesis. A
well formulated thesis not only establishes the subject of an
essay, but it indicates the direction the writer will take in
exploring the subject: as the *Handbook* states, what <u>assertion</u>
<u>about</u> that subject the writer wishes to make. For this reason,
thesis statements are also called "central" or "controlling"
ideas. Furthermore, a good thesis can provide the skeletal outline for the entire paper. If the writer's thesis statement reads,
"Television commercials appeal to our desires for good health,
good looks, and good living," the reader will expect to find paragraphs dealing with health, looks, and living in the body of the
essay. Thus, the direction of the essay has been established at
the beginning.

The ability to write a good thesis statement does not come
easily; for this reason, you will probably want to devote a great
deal of class time to it. One helpful tactic is to ask students
to write summary statements of paragraphs of other people's compositions. Exercises 31c(1-4) are particularly good for honing thesis writing skills. Oftentimes, an analysis of a student's composition from the perspective of his or her thesis statement is a
good means for checking whether the essay wanders or lacks concrete
detail and adequate development. In this connection, you may want
students to underline the thesis sentence(s) in their compositions
or to submit a thesis statement with each theme they write.

A frequent complaint of composition students is that they are
writing in a vacuum--writing artificial assignments for imaginary
readers. Sometimes this complaint is justified. As one college
senior remarked, "The only people who write freshman compositions
are freshmen. The rest of the world writes term papers, exams,
letters, memos, and reports." Nevertheless, as every composition
teacher knows, the fundamentals of writing are the same for a
business report as they are for a freshman theme. One area which
bridges the gap between compositions and "real world" writing is
audience analysis--or "considering the reader." Many composition
students assume they are writing only for their teacher. While
this is true to an extent, you should encourage them to select a
broader target audience of some sort. Section 31d can be helpful
here. Another good tactic is to ask students to include a cover
page with their essays which describes in detail the audience for
whom they are writing and which justifies their treatment of the
subject in view of that audience.

Outlining is another area you will want to emphasize, since
it requires that students think through their subject carefully
prior to writing, that they have in mind the points they intend to
discuss, and that they decide in advance the order of points for
discussion. At the same time, outlining requires that specific

points be made concerning broader aspects of the subject, and hence, encourages students to develop their essays with detailed information. Section 31e of the text can aid students in collecting a list of points on a topic, points which will later be shaped into a complete outline (see section 31g). Some instructors ask their students to submit with every composition outlines which have been developed to at least three division levels. You might also have the class hand in a detailed outline for evaluation, comment, and revision prior to the actual writing of the theme.

The type of outline used is, of course, a matter of discretion, although many instructors prefer the sentence outline for two reasons: first, it requires the student to think the subject through more thoroughly than if he or she is required to prepare a topic outline; second, a sentence outline sharpens a student's skills in composing short, precise, to-the-point sentences. Parallel structure can also be emphasized by means of the sentence outline. Tense, voice, mood, and number consistency are necessary for correct parallelism (see section 31g(4)), and these can help students achieve maximum economy and vigor of expression. You and your class will want to discuss the sample outlines provided in section 31g of the text as well as the accompanying exercises. In addition, you can add the requirement that the relevant portions of exercise 31g(1) be prepared in sentence outline form.

As was suggested in the "Larger Elements" section of this manual, a class discussion can be augmented by some group practice in outlining on the blackboard. The outline for a composition on fast food restaurant locations, given below, illustrates how one class practiced "collective" sentence outlining.

FAST FOOD: A PHENOMENON OF THE AUTO AGE

I. Introduction: The dependence of the average American upon the automobile is the key to the location of most fast food restaurants.
   A. Fifty years ago, when fewer people owned cars, families needed many services close to home.
      1. Father was the only one who regularly drove the family car--to work.
      2. Mother walked to the neighborhood grocery or dry cleaners.
      3. Children walked to school, music lessons, or the Saturday matinee.
   B. Today, many families own several cars and think nothing of driving long distances to obtain the services they need.
      1. Both father and mother may work in an industrial park or office complex far from home.
      2. Family needs such as groceries, laundry service, and medical aid are now located in shopping centers and professional buildings miles from the family's neighborhood.
      3. Children are often driven to school in a car-pool, or, if they are older, they drive their own cars.

II. The increased use of the automobile has also changed the restaurant industry.
   A. Father and mother are no longer dependent on the downtown cafe for lunch.

    1. They can drive to a restaurant far from work.
    2. They may even need a lunch spot on the fringe of the
       city; many businesses have moved to the suburbs.
  B. The family no longer does its shopping at neighborhood
     stores.
    1. Families can combine shopping and eating at spots near
       distant shopping centers.
    2. Families can eat on the way to or from running errands.
  C. Children no longer need to depend on local soda fountains
     and candy stores for snacks.
    1. They can drive to any spot in town after school.
    2. They can drive to a movie one place and drive somewhere
       else to eat afterward.

III. Conclusion: Fast food restaurants have followed the car.
  A. Fast food restaurants flourish where local traffic is
     regular and heavy.
    1. Fast food restaurants locate near industrial parks
       and office complexes.
    2. Fast food restaurants locate near outlying shopping
       and entertainment centers.
    3. Fast food restaurants locate near schools and college
       campuses.
  B. The fast food industry has also grown to fit long-
     distance travel patterns.
    1. Most people travel by car rather than public trans-
       portation when visiting relatives and friends or tak-
       ing vacations.
    2. Fast food restaurants have sprung up at interstate
       highway interchanges and along main feeder routes at
       the edge of cities.

The foregoing outline is by no means perfect, but it does
illustrate three aspects of outlining fairly well: development to
three levels, parallel structure, and relationships among main
headings and adjacent subheadings. You can point out to your class
that outlining is somewhat like a mathematical process. The subheadings under any heading or other subheading must add up to the
heading or subheadings above them: every subpoint must relate to
the part or subheading above it (e.g. I = A + (1 + 2) + B + (1 +
2). Such a procedure can very effectively bring out that proper
outlining insures that the writer keep to his or her subject.
Also, the use of subheadings requires that the various facets of
the subject be explored on a progressively more and more specific
basis--the more subheadings, the more specific the outline
becomes.

Another instructional method is to discuss from an outline,
copies of which have been provided to the students, how a paper
can be written. An outline which might be prepared for this purpose is reproduced below.

HOW TO WRITE A PAPER

  I. Introduction: Writing is important and its techniques
     warrant discussion.
    A. Writing rates in importance with reading and mathematics.
      1. Writing is performed by almost everyone in daily life.
      2. Even prople with limited educations need to know how
         to write.

B. Freshman composition will be discussed.
   1. Discussion will be focused on the 500-word theme.
   2. The three major parts of a paper, the introduction, the body, and the conclusion, will be discussed in that order.

II. Do the following things in the introduction of the paper.
   A. Catch the reader's attention by one of the following means:
      1. Show the importance of the subject,
      2. Use a startling statement or fact,
      3. Use a question,
      4. Or use a short incident or happening.
   B. Indicate the purposes of the paper.
      1. A paper has an overall purpose.
      2. A paper has a specific purpose.
   C. Signal the structure or organization of the subject matter.
      1. Indicate the parts of the subject.
      2. Indicate the order of discussion.

III. The body of the paper will involve organization and development.
   A. Consider two aspects in organization.
      1. Break the subject down into parts to be discussed.
      2. Decide the order of parts of the subject according to one of the following:
         a. Chronological order,
         b. Spatial order,
         c. Cause and effect order,
         d. Or other logical order.
   B. Develop the subject properly.
      1. Provide necessary information to make known something that is not known.
      2. Select one or more of the following means of development:
         a. Listing,
         b. Repeating,
         c. Giving examples and illustrations,
         d. Comparing,
         e. Or defining.

IV. The conclusion will involve various aspects.
   A. It will bring the composition to a close by one of two methods.
      1. Use transitional phrases such as "in conclusion."
      2. Convey through the content that the composition is being concluded.
   B. It should restate and summarize.
      1. Briefly restate the purpose of the paper.
      2. Briefly summarize the important points.
   C. It should indicate the significance of what has been described.
      1. Emphasize the importance to the reader.
      2. Emphasize the applicability of items discussed to a larger context.

V. Conclusion: The college freshman can improve his or her writing ability.

A. The purpose of this paper has been two-fold.
   1. General characteristics of expository writing have been discussed.
   2. The 500-word theme has been discussed.
B. A quick review of the steps and parts of the writing process is as follows:
   1. Select the subject.
   2. Determine the purpose for writing.
   3. Organize the subject by dividing it into its component parts and arranging these parts in logical order.
   4. In the introduction, catch the reader's attention, make the purpose for writing clear, and indicate the order of discussion.
   5. In the body, develop parts of the subject by such devices as listing, repeating, giving examples, comparing, and defining.
   6. In the conclusion, reaffirm purposes, briefly summarize important points, and indicate to the reader the significance of what has been discussed.

Students should be made aware that outline headings and sub-headings provide the springboard for further expansion--they are the skeleton upon which the composition itself is based, and the actual fleshing out of details occurs during the writing of the composition. This can be an important point, because many students will overprepare their outlines, resulting in the outline's being about as long as the finished theme--something, of course, that goes beyond the purpose of the outline.

Even though most students can see the purpose of advance preparation in other fields of endeavor, they often seem to think that for theme writing all they have to do is provide a favorable environment, invoke the muse, and by some magical method thoughts will automatically be transferred into comprehensible prose. Consequently, you may often find it necessary to prescribe some prewriting procedure. One method is to require an outline and a rough draft of a composition in advance of the final due date. Then, during a class session the student finalizes the composition, turning in at the completion of the class the finished composition, the outline, and the rough draft. This method not only insures advance preparation and prewriting but also discourages the student from turning in something other than his or her own effort.

The specimen papers at the end of section 31 can be used effectively for class discussion. You may want to divide the class into groups, have these groups critique the papers, and then have members of these groups summarize their findings for the whole class.

Exercise 31c(1)

1. Thesis is too broad and should be revised to limit discussion to one or a few aspects, e.g., "Government regulation of business causes great increases in clerical supplies and salaries."

2. Thesis needs to be better unified, e.g., "Cigarette smoking should be prohibited because it is dangerous to those who smoke."

3. Thesis is too vague. A better sentence might be "Professor Winslow is a very compassionate, understanding, and helpful instructor."

4. Thesis is too vague. A better version would be "Welfare is necessary because the ill, the elderly, and the weak must be taken care of."

5. Thesis is basically satisfactory although it would be improved if reasons why were included within it.

6. Thesis must be limited to indicate some of the qualities a good coach should possess.

7. Thesis is acceptable.

8. Thesis should be improved by subordinating the need for birth control and limiting the side-effects which will be discussed.

9. Thesis is too broad. It should be reworded to limit the aspects why the movement is important.

10. Thesis must be rewritten to make its topic more specific. The sentence should indicate some of the contributory aspects which make poverty a serious problem.

Exercise 31g(1)

THE ADVANTAGES AND DISADVANTAGES OF A CITY UNIVERSITY

Convenience of location is an advantage and hence should be handled under main heading *Advantages*. The relevance of People (IC and IIC) has to be shown better. IIB and IID are sentences and hence do not belong in a topic outline. IIIA and B apparently relate to the same thing. The relevancy of IIIC is not apparent. One way outline could be revised is as follows:

    I. Advantages
       A. Convenience of location
          1. Transportation
          2. Hotels
          3. Stores
          4. Theaters
          5. Opportunities for work
       B. Broadening of outlook
          1. Development of independence
          2. Exposure to different types of people
          3. Exposure to different ways of life

   II. Disadvantages
       A. Many distractions   A and B of course should each be
       B. Great expense   broken down into another subhead-
                                 ing.

THE VALUE OF PUBLIC OPINION POLLS

A better title would be "The Operation and Importance of Public Opinion Polls." I (Introduction) is too general to help much. With the exception of II, all items after IA3 are sentences and do not belong in a topic outline. Subheading 3 must be broken down into

79

at least two parts, but *a* as given does not relate to 3. A 2, if it is to be broken down, must be broken into at least two parts. One way outline could be revised is as follows:

    I.   Operation of public opinion polls
        A. Selection of an important issue
        B. Scientific construction of a set of questions
        C. Scientific selection of a cross section of the population
        D. Tabulation and summarization of results.

   II.   Importance of results of poll
        A. Indication of public attitudes to lawmakers
        B. Extent of people's knowledge on issue
        C. Indication of potential power of groups

BAKING YOUR OWN BREAD

All but three headings in III are sentences or lack just a subject or a verb to make them sentences. True topic headings are needed. II and III headings would be better if they emphasized difficulties of the baking in past and present. IIIB would be better handled under I. IVB, if it is to be broken down, must be broken down into at least two subheadings. One way to prepare an acceptable outline relative to this subject using essentially the parts given would be as follows:

    I.   Advantages of baking own bread
        A. Sense of satisfaction in kneading own dough
        B. Enjoyment of smell and taste
          1. Good smell of bread baking in oven
          2. Better taste of home baked bread

   II.   Differences between past and present day baking
        A. Difficulties in past
          1. Necessity to make own yeast
          2. Difficulty of kneading
          3. Necessity to bake a great deal at one time
        B. Advantages of present
          1. Availability of prepared yeast
          2. Ease of kneading
          3. Baking of only a few loaves at a time

  III.   Three easy recipes
        A. White-flour bread
        B. Whole-wheat flour bread
        C. Raisin bread

   IV.   Pleasure of eating own bread

Exercise 31h(2)

1. This beginning sentence catches the reader's interest with its humor, sets the tone of the essay, and introduces the subject of the essay effectively.

2. This statement, so unusual in a discussion of education, startles the reader and invites him to read on to find out what is to be said for a bad education.

3. The humor of the opening sentence, both in its incongruity
    and its understatement, signals to the reader that this will
    be a less than scholarly discussion of the Civil War. The
    reader is also likely to wonder what it is that causes one to
    worry about the Civil War while changing a razor blade, and
    thus he will read on.

4. Here again an unexpected assertion jars the reader's interest.

5. The technique of kicking a sacred cow, which Mr. Ciardi
    employs here, is an effective way to arouse interest.

Exercise: Specimen Papers 3 and 4

1. Specimen paper 4 is by far the better paper. Specimen paper
    3 provides a rather colorless account and fails to move the
    reader in any way. Specimen paper 4, by contrast, maintains
    an air of suspense and through some effective imagery paints
    a rather gripping word picture of what is essentially a
    rather nondescript scene.

2. "Hunting Alone" is basically arranged in a chronological
    order. However, it would be better arranged from a chrono-
    logical viewpoint if the second paragraph and the first sent-
    ence of the third paragraph were moved to the beginning of
    the paper. The organization of "The Vagrants" is arranged in
    an effective chronological manner, dealing first with the
    birds, then the man, and finally the reaction between the
    birds and the man.

3. The dominant impression of "The Vagrants" is one of gloom and
    frustration. There is a contrast between the purposeful,
    successful activity of the birds and the aimless, resentful
    activity of the men.

4. The ending of "Hunting Alone" is rather matter of fact and
    unexciting. It could be considerably improved by providing
    details which would contribute better to a sense of climax
    and surprise.

5. The beginning of "Hunting Alone" has already been commented
    upon in (1) above. The beginning of "The Vagrants" is atten-
    tion compelling and sets the stage effectively for the follow-
    ing discussion.

6. A description of the environment in which the hunting was tak-
    ing place would be in order. Selective details could greatly
    assist in reinforcing and dramatizing the events which took
    place.

EFFECTIVE PARAGRAPHS

For instructors who tackle the whole composition primarily through paragraph writing, section 32 will be extremely important. The text discusses paragraph writing under four subdivisions-- unity, coherence, development, and consistency--with major emphasis on the first three. Using the "models" approach, the *Handbook* defines and illustrates many patterns of paragraph organization including order according to time, space, climax, and general to particular (32c).

Section 32g dealing with paragraph development also addresses itself to internal order or method: development by details, examples, illustrations, or analogies, by comparison and contrast, by definition, by cause and effect, and by analysis and classifica- tion. Rather than treating thesis and support as a separate type of development, as do some composition textbooks, you may want to suggest that almost every essay has a thesis-support nature and that different methods of paragraphing are simply different approaches to adequate support of the essay's central idea.

The *Handbook* so neatly categorizes the various organizational and developmental strategies that students may become somewhat overwhelmed by illustrations and methods. While it is certainly a good idea to have them practice writing different kinds of para- graphs, it may not be wise to stress types too much at first. Instead, emphasize the overall concepts of unity and development, allowing students to expand their ideas "naturally." If you prod them with questions about their paragraph topics--"Would an illus- tration make this more clear?" "Can you give me a specific example of what you mean?" "Hadn't you better define that term?" "What can you compare it to?" "How about leading up to that observation with the events that precede it?"--you are likely to get more satisfactory results than if you predetermine the strategies to be used in writing assignments and insist the class shape their mate- rial to them. In other words, the form a paragraph takes ought to fit the content it contains rather than the other way round. Few writers say to themselves "I need a comparison here and spatial order there" before they have laid out their ideas.

Although the "models" approach is highly attractive because of its orderliness and neatness, it can mislead students into thinking that writing is a matter of preconceived, superimposed formats--something they have little confidence in their ability to achieve. Consequently, if you want your class to practice the different organizational and developmental patterns, you should be careful to use assignment material that clearly lends itself to the patterns you have in mind. The "models" approach may give instructors a lovely sense of security, but it often gives students a nasty feeling of inadequacy.

Sections 32a and 32b on the topic sentence will probably require close class discussion as the topic sentence is the key to effective paragraph unity. Once students have grasped the idea that every sentence in a paragraph must clearly relate to a dominant topic or subject aspect, their paragraphs will be much tighter.

Section 32d, with its emphasis on transition and parallelism, is particularly helpful in eliminating choppiness and that disjointed quality that often plagues student writing. Coherence frequently means little to students until they see some negative examples. Exercise 32d(3) is useful for studying coherence, but you may want to present the class with some sample paragraphs which are choppy and disjointed for reasons other than shift in person, tense, and number. Often choppy incoherence occurs because a student leaves out steps in thought, steps which tell the reader how the author's mind proceeded from point B to point D.

One of the most common problems in student essays is lack of development. Again, what seems obvious to a writer and not necessary to explain may be essential for a reader's understanding. Students who tend to write one or two sentence paragraphs need to be encouraged to "explore in depth" and even "overwrite" until they get in the habit of saying "a lot about a little."

At the end of section 32, the "Paragraphs for Study" can provide good classroom analysis and discussion. Examining the writing of professionals for main points, topic sentences, transition, methods of development and organization is always enlightening. But of course the point should always be to develop the students' own writing skills as well as their critical reading ability. Thus, the more time they spend applying section 32 to their own writing the better.

Sometimes it is effective to assign several paragraph writing sessions before the students read section 32. If you construct these assignments carefully, students will have produced many of the patterns and methods on their own. Then they can review their writing with the hindsight provided by their reading of section 32 and probably will feel less overpowered by its material. In fact, having been guided into accomplishing some of the requirements set forth in section 32 will be a boost to their confidence. For example, if you ask for several paragraphs on "what I expected to find at college and what I actually found when I arrived," students will naturally produce comparison-contrast material; however, if you ask for a "comparison-contrast paragraph on college life" you are likely to get stumbling, sweaty-palmed results and a high degree of student frustration.

Exercise 32a

1. First sentence.

2. First sentence.

3. Combination of third and fourth sentences: "Today's bright and serious students are always putting administrators on the spot because they want to put the knowledge of the past to work in the present and to make the educational process provide a continuum between ideas and social and political action.

4. First sentence.

1. Sentences 4, 5, and 6.

2. Sentences 2 and 3. If sentence 2 is deleted, sentence 3 with
    the *so* deleted can follow sentence 1.

3. Sentence 5.

4. Sentences 5 and 6. However, by using an appropriate transi-
    tional tense, sentence 6 can be made to follow logically
    sentence 1.

5. Sentence 4, 5, and 6.

6. Sentences 3 and 6.

Exercise 32b(2)

1. Given my choice, I would sooner be in the Air Force than any
    other service because I am more interested in flying than in
    any other military occupation. Opportunities for advancement
    are also greater in the Air Force. Finally, wages in certain
    brackets of the Air Force are higher than in other branches.

2. The wreck on Route 64 at Mt. Nixon was caused entirely by
    carelessness and reckless driving by the driver of the Buick.
    When the wreck occurred, the lights were green for the cars
    coming off the side road. A heavy truck loaded with hay was
    pulling out to cross the highway. The Buick came speeding
    down the main road, went through the stoplight, and crashed
    back into the truck.

3. We owe some of our notions of radar to scientific observations
    of bats. Scientists noticed that bats rarely collided with
    anything in their erratic flight. Keen eyesight could not be
    the reason for their flying the way they do since bats are
    blind. It was found that bats keep sending out noises inaud-
    ible to people and that they hear the echoes of those noises.
    This principle whereby they fly safely was found to be similar
    to the main principle of radar.

Exercise 32c(1)

Thomas Hardy, English novelist, short story writer, and poet,
is considered one of the most important of the writers who revolted
against Victorian tradition at the end of the nineteenth century.
A pessimist, he presented in his work important novels--*The Return
of the Native, Tess of the D'Urbervilles,* and *Jude the Obscure*--
studies of life in the bleak English countryside. In these studies,
individuals äre defeated in their struggle against their physical
and social environment and the caprices of chance. In 1928, he
died at the age of eighty-eight.

Exercise 32c(2)

Landing a space capsule on Mars is technically complicated.
Descending through Martian atmosphere is much trickier than landing

on the airless moon. The Soviets tried to land on Mars four times, twice in 1971 and twice in 1974. In 1971 one Soviet lander crashed and another stopped sending signals back after twenty seconds. One of the Soviet 1974 attempts just flew past Mars. Instruments on the second 1974 flight failed during descent after transmitting usable signals for a few seconds.

We use spoken and written language to express the meaning we want to convey. Language is full of symbols, but we also use signs or images that are not strictly descriptive. Some of these signs are mere abbreviations or strings of initials such as UN or UNESCO. Other signs are things such as familiar trademarks, badges, flags, and traffic lights. Although meaningless in themselves, signs have acquired a recognizable meaning through common usage or deliberate intention. Such things are not symbols. They are signs and do no more than denote the object to which they are attached.

Juvenile delinquency is a major problem in this country. Everywhere we read and hear about the vicious crimes committed by younger people. Many of them are organized in gangs and are proud of their devotion to a life of crime. Certainly this unfortunate situation grows partly out of the years of World War II. For one thing, the war inspired brutality in the young generation by distorting and twisting humane values. The newspapers and the movies depicted violence, cruelty, and bloodletting as heroic rather than vicious. For another, parents of youngsters born during the war either avoided their responsibilities or were unable to exercise them. Many fathers were in the service; mothers were often busy working in war plants. The result was an unhappy, undisciplined group of young people. It is no wonder they soon made a problem of themselves.

Exercise 32d(1)

Many students foolishly object to taking courses in writing. Their notion, however, that only poets, novelists, and newspaper workers have to know how to write is unrealistic. As an example, a student going into the technical or scientific fields may think that writing is something he seldom has to do, but practicing engineers and scientists say they spend half their time writing letters and reports. Similarly, college students going into business think their secretaries will do their writing for them. Unfortunately, not only does this attitude show a naive faith in the compentency of secretaries, but it fails to take into account that young businessmen seldom have secretaries, competent or otherwise. Factors such as these would seemingly indicate, other things being equal, that a man in any field who can express himself effectively is sure to succeed more rapidly than a man whose command of language is poor.

Exercise 32d(2)

Radio amateurs, or hams, send messages on their home radio stations to people all over the world. Despite the fact that it takes a considerable amount of equipment to operate a ham radio, there are 260,000 licensed amateur stations in the United States. One of them is operated by my cousin, Glenn Wade, who once had D.R.T. as his signal code which he used to broadcast as "Dirty Rotten Tomatoes." There are four types of licensed hams may obtain from the FCC: (1) novice, (2) technician, (3) general class, and (4) extra class. Although their major purpose is recreation, the Federal Communications Commission has often praised these hams for their voluntary aid in times of emergency such as floods or storms.

Exercise 32d(3)

1. Literature is a medium through which a person can convey his ideas toward or protests against different norms of society. A work that deals with a moral issue is of particular importance in literature; it is written with a particular purpose in mind. A literary work with a moral issue, such as a Shakespearean play, lives on to be reinterpreted by different generations. Such a work involves the reader, for he forms his own moral judgment toward the issue. Arthur Miller's *Death of a Salesman* is a play which deals with a moral issue.

2. It is difficult to feel compassion for a person who does not deserve it. My neighbor, John Carroll, is a poor little rich boy who just can't find happiness and love. He has never been deprived of anything but the one thing he really wanted: a girl who had gone to high school with him--a girl he couldn't get. His mother tells the story in such a way that it is easy to feel pity for this man because of this one thing that he couldn't attain. A person who least deserves compassion gets more than his share of it.

3. Every time a nation is involved in a war, it must face problems about its ex-soldiers after that war. Veterans are entitled to some special considerations from society, but treating them with complete fairness is a baffling problem. Livy reports that grants to former soldiers caused some troubles in the early history of Rome. There were many disagreements between them and the early Roman senators.

4. Preparing a surface for new paint is as important a step in the whole process as the application of the paint itself. First, be sure that the surface is quite clean. Wash any grease or grime from the woodwork. Use turpentine or a detergent for this. Be careful to clean off whatever cleanser is used. Then sand off any rough or chipped paint.

5. One of the books I read in high school English was Dickens's *Tale of Two Cities*. In it the author tells of some of the horrors of the French Revolution. He spends several pages telling about how the French aristocrats suffer. The climax of the book tells how a ne'er-do-well who had failed in life sacrifices himself for another. He takes his place in a prison and goes stoically to the guillotine for him.

Exercise 32f(1)

Frederick Winslow Taylor was born in 1856. Fred's father was a lawyer. His mother was a cultured Easterner. She took the family abroad for three years. While at Exeter, Fred was a star baseball player and head of his class. He was short, heavily built, and sharp-tongued.

Fred began work as a machinist. He liked the men he worked with. He thought up new ways of doing things. When he became a foreman, he forgot about his working pals. He divided up jobs. In six years he became chief engineer. The idea of efficiently producing things went to his head. He lectured on production techniques at various colleges. Then he went to work for Bethlehem Steel. This job did not last long. The reason he lost his job was that he was more interested in production than in profit.

When he was thirty-four, he married. He began to play golf and entertain. He died in 1915 of pneumonia. He was one of the first efficiency experts.

Exercise 32g(1)

1. Details, examples, and illustrations; comparison and contrast

2. Details, examples, and illustrations; comparison and contrast

3. Comparison and contrast; definition; illustration

4. Details, examples, and illustrations; repetition and restatement; explanation of causes and effects

5. Details, examples and illustrations; explanation of causes and effects

6. Chronological order; explanation of causes and effects

7. Chronological order; explanation of causes and effects

8. Spatial order; explanation of causes and effects

9. Comparison and contrast; illustration; causes and effects

10. Chronological order; details, examples, and illustrations; repetition and restatement

11. Repetition and restatement; explanation of causes and effects

12. Details, examples, and illustrations; comparison and contrast; explanation of causes and effects

13. Comparison and contrast; definition; examples and illustrations

14. Details, examples, and illustrations; definition

15. Comparison and contrast, explanation of causes and effects

16. Details, examples, and illustrations; comparison and contrast; repetition and restatement

17. Explanation of causes and effects; illustrations and examples

18. Details, examples, and illustrations; comparison and contrast; explanation of causes and effects

19. Comparison and contrast; definition, explanation of causes and effects

20. Details, examples, and illustrations; comparison and contrast

Exercise 32h(1)

1. Macleish's tone is dramatic and portentous. He uses devices
   of parallel structure and anthithesis and a striking allusion
   to Peter's betrayal of Christ to achieve a strong sense of
   urgency and a presentiment of disaster if what he proposes is
   not fulfilled. The aspect of a time of reckoning being near
   at hand is forcefully emphasized and re-emphasized by repeated
   assertion of failure to take positive action.

2. Krutch's tone is serious, contemplative, and touched with
   regret. After making several statements about man's nature
   ("It is not easy to live..."; "The faculty of wonder tires
   easily..."), he suggests in the last sentence the need for
   determination ("almost inevitably to have to try it") to
   achieve what, "alas," is so very difficult to achieve.

3. Mr. Gass's tone is informal and contains a strong recurring
   note of resignation which awards hysteria but which seems all
   the more ominous because of his matter-of-fact mode of presentation. He achieves an aspect of quiet despair by amassing
   a number of details tying in each observation to the color of
   hopelessness--gray. His final conclusion, that "everyone is
   out of luck who lives here," only serves by way of understate-
   ment to more poignantly accentuate the deplorable fate of
   those who live in the area he describes.

4. Churchill is addressing an audience that is certain of the
   rightness of the cause of freedom but wants to be inspired
   to heroic resistance. In the long series of parallel structures, the powerful repetition of "we shall fight," and the
   periodic final clause, we hear the strong voice of the representative man of freedom and the determined leader of a besieged nation.

5. Typical of Faulkner's style, this passage suggests both nos-
   talgia for the fresh, exciting day of Ike's youth and sorrow
   for the disappearance of the frontier. The sentence structure
   attempts to recreate the thought process of an old man remem-
   bering his youthful response to life.

SECTIONS 33-36

EFFECTIVE SENTENCES

Sections 33-36 examine sentence structure from a rhetorical rather than a grammatical perspective. After having achieved grammatical correctness, students usually turn their attention from sentences to the larger elements of the composition. However, their writing will lack power and verve unless they devote some attention to sentence effectiveness. As the basic structural element of writing, the sentence is responsible for communicating the logical development of thought. In addition, the sentence can be used to achieve specific effects, to indicate nuances, to place emphasis. The sections in the *Handbook* discuss subordination, variety, parallelism, and emphasis as tools for achieving logic, precision, and impact in sentences.

It has been said that the best type of writing is unobtrusive, that is, writing which provides a smooth roadway over which the writer's thoughts are transmitted in a seemingly effortless manner. In such an instance, the reader is often not conscious of the writing as such because it is accomplishing its basic mission, that of conveying the writer's message. In other words, the reader is not distracted by the writing; he is able to concentrate fully upon assimilating the content. His comment, then, as he reviews writing of this type will focus on the clarity, precision, and directness of the development, all of which of course is really a tribute to the quality of the writing, since it has achieved the purpose of good expository writing--that of explaining clearly and persuasively.

The reader, then, appreciates the fact that information is clearly imparted but generally will not be concerned with determining how the overall effect has been produced. Were he to do so, he would find in large part that the writing has become what it is because of the way in which the sentences were constructed. He would find presentations of clear, smooth cause-effect relationships; skillful coordination and subordination; variety of sentence structure; the accurate and clear utilization of connectives and sentences which vary in length. He would also discover parallel structure; sentence thought arrangements leading up to an emphasis on main ideas at the end of sentences; and skillful use of active or passive voice, depending upon what the writer has desired to stress--the actor or the action.

In short, the good writer must be a good craftsman; and unless he is a good craftsman with sentences, it is unlikely that his overall writing effort will impress. It is true that it is the interaction of the parts which results in a smooth functioning of the whole.

Effective sentences are really a matter of style, and your students will doubtless feel you are asking a bit much of them-- they are likely to feel that correct grammar and coherence are

certainly enough effort. However, many students have never studied
sentence effectiveness in any detail, and while they will complain
that they "are not Shakespeare," most are fascinated to learn how
sentences can be constructed and manipulated to achieve particular
stress and emphasis. You may not see many immediate results of
this new knowledge in their own writing--their goal will probably
still be just to "get it down on paper"--but the time spent on
sections 33-36 is nevertheless time well spent.

SECTIONS 33-34

SUBORDINATION AND VARIETY

Section 33, which deals with subordination, contains several good exercises to assist students in understanding the uses of subordination. You will probably find it beneficial to point out that subordination is closely tied to the logical relationships of ideas in sentences: ideas of equal, greater, and lesser importance are ranked and stressed by means of correct coordination and subordination. Subordination can also be used to express cause and effect relationships. Exercises 33a-d provide valuable practice in aligning major and minor ideas properly through correct subordination.

Section 34, on variety, explains the proper use of short and long sentences, how to avoid monotony. Exercise 34c allows students to use several sentence patterns to achieve greater sentence variety.

Exercise 33a

1. Because I didn't see the traffic light, I didn't stop.

2. Because the city's sanitation workers are striking, the garbage has not been collected for two weeks.

3. Although the Indian Highway was formerly an Indian trail, since it is a major highway, it is a scenic as well as an important route.

4. In addition to several broken bottles, her grandfather's will left her a collection of old glass, three clocks, and an antique car.

5. Although pollution and overpopulation are our most serious problems, we are spending billions on new weapons.

6. His father, who had moved to New York in 1967, was an accountant and worked for the City Bank.

7. Although Olsen bought his new car only three months ago, he has already had two accidents.

8. James Dickey, who was born in 1923, has written the novel *Deliverance* and several books of poems.

9. He had dropped out of high school but he decided to get a job. When he couldn't find one, he decided to go back to school. Later, he went on to college.

10. *Funny Girl*, which had a long run on Broadway, broke many box office records. It was later made into a movie in which

91

Barbra Streisand played the leading role.

Exercise 33b

1. As we drove onto a narrow gravel road leading into the woods, we wondered whether it was safe.

2. The house, which was very old, had faded yellow paint that was cracked in some places.

3. Since the bookshelves were too expensive, I went to a lumber yard, bought some boards and brackets, and put bookshelves up myself.

4. Because I got up late this morning and had to wait for a bus, I was late to class.

5. Robert Fulton, one of the early experimenters with submarines, built the first successful steamboat and also experimented with torpedoes.

6. Although he had never smoked marijuana before, when he was invited to a pot party, he went. When someone offered him a "reefer," he took it but since the effect was not quite what he had expected, he didn't finish it and left the party.

7. Late-night TV talk shows are very popular. The host is usually very funny and talks about various things with the guests, some of whom are politicians and show-business celebrities, who are from many walks of life. The mixture makes for interesting conversation.

8. TV documentaries, which are very interesting, have showed the plight of the migrant workers, conditions in the ghetto, and the helplessness of our neglected senior citizens. The one I liked best was entitled "Birth and Death."

9. She decided to take the subway, but since she didn't know the way, she asked directions of the travel agent, who was very helpful.

10. Although I studied hard, read the textbook and outside sources, wrote a fifteen-page paper, and bought the instructor a Christmas present, I flunked the course.

Exercise 33c-d

1. By pulling the emergency cord, she averted a train wreck.

2. According to the popular ballad, Casey Jones's attempt to arrive on schedule was prevented by a head-on collision with another train.

3. The reporters, many of them wearing their presscards pinned to their lapels, flocked to the launch site. There the technicians were giving a last check to the spaceship. It was to carry three astronauts, who were just then walking up the ramp, to the moon.

4. Ralph Waldo Emerson, an individualist, said "Whoso would be a man must be a nonconformist."

5. *A Clockwork Orange*, written by Anthony Burgess and a best seller for many months, was made into a motion picture. Directed by Stanley Kubrick, it was very well received by film critics who thought it was one of the year's best movies.

6. Although prices continued to rise, his salary remained the same.

7. When Mrs. Wood opened the door of the cage, her pet parrot escaped.

8. I bought my sports car from a friend of mine, a car enthusiast who buys old cars and then rebuilds them as a hobby. My car has developed a rumble in the engine which has begun to worry me, for I know nothing about repairing cars and haven't the money to go to a mechanic.

9. Although he fell seven stories, breaking eight ribs and puncturing one lung, he lived to tell the tale.

10. Although Marion had to pay most of her own expenses, she graduated with honors.

Exercise 33e

1. Ann likes her coffee black, but I like cream in mine.

2. I did not feel that I was qualified for the job.

3. My parents bought a new car although they still liked the old one.

4. She was dead tired, and so she lay down to rest.

5. Although it was very cold, he continued to work.

6. I don't really feel that I should go out in this weather--not with the cold I have.

7. When the ship struck the rocks, several people jumped overboard.

8. He talks as though he is happy.

9. I don't know whether I can paint since I have never tried.

10. When the furnace broke down, the manager closed the offices.

Exercise 34c

1. After fighting traffic for an hour and a half we came home. *OR* Sullen and irritable we were when we came home after fighting traffic for an hour and a half.

2. Although the child had lost her way, she was brought home by a thoughtful neighbor. *OR* Brought home by a thoughtful neighbor was the child who had lost her way.

93

3. To protest the umpire's decision, the coach rushed out on
    the field. *OR* Protesting the umpire's decision, the coach
    rushed out on the field.

4. Because his head ached and his mouth felt dry, he knew his
    hangover had begun. *OR* His head aching and his mouth feel-
    ing dry, he knew his hangover had begun.

5. Stretching and fastening the chair cover with amazing speed
    was the upholsterer with his mouth full of tacks and his
    magnetic hammer swinging like a piece of machinery. *OR* And
    the upholsterer, his mouth full of tacks and his magnetic
    hammer swinging like a piece of machinery, stretched and
    fastened the chair cover with amazing speed.

6. Since the Surgeon General has determined that cigarette smok-
    ing is dangerous to your health, heed that warning which is
    printed on every package of cigarettes. *OR* Determining that
    cigarette smoking is dangerous to your health, the Surgeon
    General has printed that warning on every package of cigar-
    ettes.

7. Because the earthquake caused much loss of life and devasta-
    tion in the villages and cities of Nicaragua, the United
    States quickly offered assistance. *OR* There was much loss
    of life and devastation in the villages and cities of Nicar-
    agua, and so the United States quickly offered assistance.

8. Making important contributions to American literature for
    more than 150 years are Black writers, but many educated
    people are still not aware of it. *OR* Although Black writers
    have made important contributions to American literature for
    more than 150 years, many educated people are still not aware
    of it.

9. Wanting to dance, they viewed the broken record player. *OR*
    There was the broken record player and with them wanting to
    dance.

10. By refinishing only old furniture which they bought, they
    were able to furnish their new home at relatively little
    cost. *OR* At relatively little cost, they were able to fur-
    nish their new home because they bought only old furniture
    which they refinished themselves.

Exercise 34a-c

The following is, of course, only one of many possible re-
writings.

As he slammed the front door, Mark felt better. He did not
even glance over his shoulder to see if his parents were watching
him. After walking to a nearby park, he sat down on the bench.
Why his parents had yelled at him he knew very well. And he did-
n't blame them. They had both worked hard at their restaurant to
keep him in comfort. They wanted him to have the opportunities
that they had missed. They wanted him to become a doctor. But
he couldn't seem to concentrate at school. Although he liked most
of his teachers, he didn't really hear them and just wanted to
sleep in class. There was no denying that the marks he brought

home were very poor. But he didn't want to be a doctor; he wanted
to work with automobiles. The smell of gasoline, the sound of the
motor, the shine of the chrome--those were the things that fascinated him. Tell them the truth, he thought. How can I be something I don't want to be? But he delayed returning home. He did
not look forward to the scene they would make and the lack of
understanding they would show.

PARALLELISM

Clear, direct, forceful, and to-the-point sentences are often achieved with parallelism--an important technique for establishing logical relationships and emphasis. Some uses of parallelism have been discussed as part of the section on outlining. But beyond outlining and general applications to expository prose, parallelism plays a key role in writing situations students may face later in business and industry. For example, well written management reports use titles, headings, and captions presented in parallel form. Training manuals and performance instructions list procedures in parallel construction to help readers keep track of the steps in a process. Parallelism is used as a cue in many situations where clarity and exactness are crucial.

In addition, effective parallelism increases our enjoyment of all kinds of communication. Authors and speech makers have long known that parallelism strikes with special force and satisfies our desire for symmetry. Caesar's words "I came, I saw, I conquered" are remembered today. Certainly no one would quote him if he had said, "When I got there, I looked around and then defeated the opposition."

One of the most famous of all books--the Holy Bible--fairly rebounds with parallel structure; and classes are often intrigued by a discussion of passages from the Bible illustrating how parallel structure assists biblical writers in achieving the powerful, hammering effect so characteristic of this great work. There are so many good passages in the Bible to illustrate this particular effect that it is rather presumptuous to recommend any single one. Nevertheless, many students have found the Book of Ecclesiastes to be especially fascinating, and the first chapter of Ecclesiastes is an extremely appealing one. Such lines as "The sun also ariseth, and the sun goeth down and hasteth to the place where he arose" and "The thing that hath been it is that which shall be: and that which is done is that which shall be done"; and "there is no new thing under the sun" offer all sorts of opportunities for a fruitful discussion concerning how parallel structure assists the "gentle skeptic" in achieving his wistful, memorable account of the futility of all things mortal.

Exercise 35a

1. His work consisted of planning the menus, purchasing the food, and supervising the employees.

2. He bought a new Volvo having a standard transmission and a radio and heater.

3. The lecture was long, tiresome, and not easily understood.

4. The biography of Stilwell is interesting, lively, and also informative.

5. Being too early, even if it wastes valuable time, is better than arriving late.

6. Mary has a full-time job, is a member of the school committee, and does her own housework.

7. The student was told to obtain a transcript of his grades and then to apply for admission.

8. To be a good teacher, one must be patient, like to help others, and show an infinite capacity for learning.

9. The policeman told us to drive very slowly and not to put on our bright lights.

10. Marcia moved to a new apartment with more space and air conditioning.

Exercise 35c

1. A good politician not only works well with people but also does not compromise his ideals.

2. Hemingway was both a good writer and an influence on other writers.

3. The reviewer couldn't decide whether to ignore the book or write an unfavorable review.

4. Either Congress will repeal the law or the Supreme Court will declare it unconstitutional.

5. He was both intelligent and courteous.

SECTION 36

EMPHASIS

The exercises in section 36 stress emphasis through placement of sentence elements, arrangement of sentence elements in proper order, repetition of sentence elements, and use of active and passive voices. Your class may enjoy reading some prose passages from seventeenth-century authors such as John Donne and Sir Thomas Browne, whose sermons and essays illustrate the adept use of loose and periodic sentences. Another excellent source of well constructed prose is *Vital Speeches of the Day*, a collection of major speeches by American public figures, found in the periodical room of most libraries. Passages from presidential inaugural addresses often contain good sentences for illustrating subordination, variety, and emphasis. At the very least, your students' ability to enjoy effective prose and their understanding of the source of that enjoyment will be increased.

The "effective sentences" Review Exercise at the end of section 36 provides a good test of student perceptiveness in identifying causes of ineffective sentences and the rewording of such sentences to achieve increased vigor, power, and emphasis.

Exercise 36a

1. In my opinion, he is an overbearing, egotistical bore.

2. By and large, the results of the flood were disastrous.

3. As a rule, women are more perceptive and far more sensitive then men are.

4. Tolstoy had, for the most part, a profound understanding of people and of the passions that drive them.

5. If I had my way, this university would be closed and its faculty fired.

6. Teddy Roosevelt, I have read, was dynamic and full of life.

7. Test results prove, in most cases, that smoking seriously impairs the health.

8. It seems to me that the lawyer shirked his responsibility and the judge was biased.

9. The day was clear, the sun was shining, and the snow was packed hard; in my opinion, it was a great day for skiing.

10. With its superior technology and its single-minded determination, if everything goes right, the U.S. will definitely win the space race.

Exercise 36b

1. After her marriage broke up, she began seeing a psychiatrist regularly.

2. After his first business failed, he started a new business and made a million dollars.

3. Although we tried to keep it in a cool place, the wine turned to vinegar.

4. The rowers bending rhythmically and the oars flashing in the sun, the boat neared the finish line.

5. Stamping their feet and blowing on their fingers, they stood the cold for an hour.

6. Several years ago on a three-lane highway in Minnesota, I saw two cars crash head-on.

7. After she suffered a severe depression, her doctor insisted that she take a vacation.

8. If, after you have finished typing it, the footnotes are in good order, your research paper will be accepted.

9. Although she had checked her figures and added again, Norma still had not balanced her accounts.

10. Between the ship and the shore lay three miles of rough water.

Exercise 36c

1. He moved away from the city because he wanted to let his dog run, his rent was high, and he was ill.

2. Most students get bored with school after years of elementary school, high school, and college.

3. She inherited some jewelry, a house, and a million dollars.

4. The play received terrible reviews and closed after the first week.

5. The candidate smiled at the children, mingled with men in the street, and promised a guaranteed income for all.

6. Charles is a poker player, a capable gardener, and a famous doctor. (If an anticlimax is intended, sentence can be left as given.)

7. We find similar psychological reactions in frogs, rats and guinea pigs to those of men.

8. During his vacation David acquired a bad sunburn, some souvenirs, and a wife. (If an anticlimax is intended, it might be written as follows: David acquired a wife, some souvenirs, and a bad sunburn.)

9. The earthquake toppled several of the buildings in the area and caused 100 deaths.

10. Laurence Olivier is a director and producer as well as being one of the great Shakespearean actors of all time.

Exercise 36e

1. A skillful thrower can make a boomerang do amazing stunts.

2. An angry dog snapped at my ankles.

3. The radiator of her car froze during the cold spell.

4. We must exercise extreme caution if we are to experiment with genetic change.

5. The press scrutinized police procedures.

6. My parents planned an addition to the house.

7. The reporters interviewed the returned astronauts.

8. The chairman of the refreshments committee selected the menu.

9. Drunken drivers cause many major accidents.

10. The local Department of Health distributes polio vaccine.

"Effective Sentences" Review Exercise

(Sections 33-36)

1. SUB - Although Mario was still deeply in debt, he felt that the bargain was too good to let pass.

2. SUB - Because the child was terrified and confused, he fell exhausted on the wet leaves.

3. SUB, COOR - Robert Frost, a poet, wrote about rural New England and the human condition.

4. PAR - After reading the book, Susan decided to change her way of life and her p ans for the future.

5. SUB - Although the fighter was very strong and in excellent condition, he was knocked out in the fifth round.

6. EMP - It is a shame that poverty still exists in The United States because we are the wealthiest nation on earth, there is no excuse for it, and it's about time we eradicated it.

7. EMP - India and Pakistan are but two examples of the many countries suffering from overpopulation.

8. PAR - Some college students regard their education as irrelevant and not useful.

9. SUB - After working in the Peace Corps for two years and after refusing several job offers, Elizabeth returned to school.

10. PAR - He leaned back in his chair, closed his eyes, rested his hands on his lap, and went to sleep.

11. EMP - While Chekhov attended medical school, he wrote short stories to support his family.

12. SUB, PAR - The substitute teacher, a married woman with a good sense of humor, conveyed her ardent love of science to her classes.

13. PAR - To a naughty child, a scolding parent seems like a giant standing seven feet tall with a large mouth and eyes that glare in the dark.

14. SUB - Not only our love of Colonial arts and crafts but also our love of modern technological skills is reflected in our homes and magazines.

15. SUB - In Arizona, the state with the largest Indian population, live the Hopi, Navajo, and Apache.

16. PAR - To become a responsible voter, you should know the issues, listen to the candidates, become familiar with their views, learn their weaknesses, and come to know their strengths. Then you can make a wise choice.

17. SUB - When Rachel Carson wrote a great deal about the dangers of insecticides, she was vigorously opposed by insecticide companies and by people who find insecticides helpful. But what about the people who have been poisoned by them?

18. SUB - Harlem, which is infested with rats and disease, is reached by walking up Fifth Avenue, the most glamorous street in the richest city in the world.

19. EMP - A movie was made that recalled those days when the Boston Strangler roamed free and terror gripped the city of Boston.

20. SUB - One reason that the space trip was an unqualified success was that the astronauts had been kept in seclusion for weeks before it to guard them against infection.

LOGIC

Composition instructors frequently complain that before they can teach their students how to write, they have to teach them how to think. Typically, student papers proceed from hasty generalization to hasty generalization with little or no supporting evidence to validate sweeping conclusions. These same papers may exhibit little awareness of cause and effect, poor organization, and faulty analysis of the topic under discussion. Because students often do not know how to think through an issue and draw valid conclusions, let alone write meaningfully about that issue, a good case can be made for dealing with the material in section 37 at an early stage in your course. Logical thinking is essential to all types of writing, and the first composition should be, if it is a good one, one that is logically reasoned.

On the other hand, you may feel that other matters of grammar and construction are more important at the time of the first writing assignments, and you may wish to postpone logic until more pressing aspects of writing have been covered. If your course is structured to treat argumentation in the second term, as is the case in many composition programs, you may decide to reserve a detailed discussion of logic until that time.

As the *Handbook* notes, section 37 contains an abbreviated overview of definitions, generalizations, and a few of the more common logical fallacies. Although the discussions of informal and formal definitions and hasty, unsubstantiated generalizations are thorough, if you plan an in-depth treatment of fallacies, you will probably want to supplement the text with a more complete list from another source. The *Handbook* emphasizes cause-effect relationships and valid conclusions through an examination of the *post hoc, ergo propter hoc* fallacy, the *non-sequitur,* begging the question, false analogies, and false dilemmas. The text also discusses prejudicial language (connotation, "fear" words, and "glitter" terms), *argumentum ad hominem,* transfer techniques, and *argumentum ad populum* ("bandwagon").

Because any one of several fallacies may contribute to illogical statements, or generalizations err in several directions, or definitions be constructed in several ways, the following answers for exercises in section 37 should be viewed as suggestions rather than dictates.

Exercise 37a(1)

1. The class to which the term belongs is named, but it is too broad. The definition does not differentiate the term from other things in the class, i.e., a woman. The term being defined is not repeated, and it is stated in parallel form.

2. The definition is not parallel in form. As such, it has no
    class and in effect uses the term being defined in its defini-
    tion.

3. No class is established. As such, the statement indicates a
    purpose of the thermometer but does not define it.

4. The statement is an opinion, not a definition. The term be-
    ing defined is not established as a member of a class.

5. The statement is not parallel in structure. As such, no class
    is established. Basically, the term being defined is used in
    the attempted definition.

6. The statement does not relate what is being defined to a class.

7. The statement is not parallel in structure. As such, there is
    no class established.

8. This statement assigns the term being defined to a class, but
    as a definition, it fails because it does not clearly differ-
    entiate the term being defined from others in the class, e.g.,
    a baking pan.

9. No class is established.

10. This statement has a class, *place*. However, the definition
    could apply just as well to a jail or prison.

Exercise 37a(2)

1. A raincheck is an offer, usually in writing, to provide ser-
    vices or merchandise at a later time.

2. A guerilla is a warrior who is a member of an irregular
    fighting force.

3. A juke box is a coin-operated electric phonograph which pro-
    vides recorded music when selector buttons are pushed.

4. A chair is a piece of furniture having a seat, back, and legs,
    designed for one person.

5. An examination is an inquiry which seeks to determine answers
    to questions and the extent of compliance with standards.

Exercise 37b

1. It is sometimes difficult for women who have children to work
    and still care properly for their children.

2. Many thoughtful people believe that television is responsible
    for much of the violence of today.

3. Some intelligent people cannot believe in religion in the
    twentieth century.

4. In many instances, a college education can increase earning
    power.

5. There are some people who believe that inflation is caused by a small number of greedy corporations.

6. Some women who support women's liberation are frustrated and unsuccessful.

7. There are some who believe that anyone who gets to be head of a large corporation has to be ruthless and materialistic.

8. Some people believe that lobbies discourage honest legislation.

9. Many believe that welfare discourages people from seeking employment.

10. The question that has to be asked here is "successful in what respect?" Or, the question could be asked, "more successful than whom?"

Exercise 37c

1. Prejudgment. The fact that movie stars are goodlooking is not in itself a reason for unsuccessful marriages. Investigation into many movie star marriages would have to be made before any valid conclusions could be reached as to whether such marriages are generally unhappy or the reasons therefore if the case were such.

2. Transfer. What is true of an individual is not necessarily true of the government which has financial resources available that an individual does not have. The statement under discussion also rests upon an anlogy and could be developed into an argument from analogy.

3. Transfer. Attitudes of an ancient people are in many respects not the same as those of a modern people. Also, even where punishment is involved, modes of punishment vary greatly over the years.

4. Bandwagon. Politicians are sometimes held in low esteem and many people don't need much convincing that what politicians do is wrong.

5. *Argumentum ad hominem.* Although one may not approve of a person because he is an athiest, the fact that he is an athiest doesn't mean that he can't teach.

6. Transfer. The word *pampered* has an undesirable connotation as far as many people are concerned and identifying college students as pampered children prejudices many people against them.

7. *Argumentum ad hominem.* The fact that the man was a criminal doesn't necessarily mean he is now criminally inclined.

8. Prejudgment based upon a hasty generalization. What one Paris hotel did is not necessarily indicative of what the French in general do.

9. Bandwagon. Many people believe black people to be naturally
    rhythmic because of the great success of many black musicians.
    However, many other blacks would have to be considered before
    blacks in general could be so regarded.

10. Prejudgment and *argumentum ad hominem*. Most people don't like
    draft resisters, but the reason for some individuals resisting
    the draft may not be that they are afraid to die for their
    country but, rather, that they question the cause for which
    they might have to die were they to be drafted.

Exercise 37d

1. Begging the question

2. *Post hoc*

3. *Non Sequitur*

4. *Non Sequitur*

5. False analogy

6. *Non Sequitur*

7. *Non Sequitur*

8. *Non Sequitur*

9. *Post hoc*

10. *Post hoc*

In dealing with illogical statements, one problem is that all
examples of fallacious reasoning are *non sequiturs* in that their
conclusions do not follow from their premises. Begging the question may be an exception to this, but both false analogy and *post
hoc* fallacies are *non sequiturs*; thus, all of these, with the possible exception of the first, may be accurately judged to be *non
sequiturs*, though 5 is also a false analogy and 2, 9, and 10 are also *post hoc* fallacies.

"Logic" Review Exercise 37-A

Both speakers fail to develop a logical argument. Mr. Jones
uses charged language instead of clearly defined terms. His
generalizations are hasty and overstated, and he concludes his remarks with a *non sequitur*. Mr. Smith responds with a false analogy,
an *ad hominem*, an overstated generalization, a *non sequitur* and in
effect does not deal with the problem of the standards of literacy
and journalism Mr. Jones is concerned about.

"Logic" Review Exercise 37-B

The selection abounds with *argumentum ad hominems*. The first
paragraph contains several vilificatory comments about sports-
writers: "These tin-horn sports," "these semiliterate dealers in
clichés," "misinformation and moronic opinions." The second paragraph attacks sportswriters as lacking objectivity and penetration.

Several good examples are provided which indicate sportswriters' lack of penetration, but the writer offers no proof that sports-writers are not objective. Obviously the sportswriter has to tell who won and, in the last analysis, if a team won it must have played a better game at least as far as the final score is concerned. Stating that a team's supporters wanted to win is neither irrelevant nor vicious although it might be considered a self-evident fact.

More name-calling takes place in the third paragraph. There can be little doubt that a great deal of small talk takes place during the description of a football game and that many clichés are uttered such as "the game isn't over until the final gun sounds." But a football game is not staged with the idea of providing high level intellectual activity for the viewer. In the last analysis, the writer would have done better had he eschewed personal invective and concentrated upon some constructive criticism as to how the game could have been described more graphically for the viewer.

WORDS

Of all the sections in a handbook, the one on words is probably the least frequently assigned. This is not surprising, given
the number of writing problems you and your class must tackle during a term. Many instructors naturally rank word study rather low
on their list of imperatives.

However, if you wish to make some corrective efforts on be-
half of vocabulary, diction, and spelling, there are several alter-
natives. One, of course, is assigning all or portions of sections
38-44. At the other end of the scale, you can instruct your students to keep lists of words they use incorrectly or misspell in
their compositions. And if you are ambitious, you can work up a
testing system to insure that they are learning proper usage and
spelling. Simply marking word errors when they occur in compositions usually does very little to prevent students from making the
same errors again, other than bringing these errors momentarily to
their attention.

Or, as a third alternative, you can intersperse word study
among other assignments throughout the semester. This approach
often succeeds well because "word work" becomes a relatively regular event and may even be viewed by students as a pleasant break in
routine. One instructor achieved good results by scheduling fif-
teen minutes each week as "learn-a-word time." At the beginning
of each session she presented a few Greek or Latin prefixes, suffixes, and roots, explained their meanings, and asked the class to
list on the board as many words as they could think of that included them. In succeeding classes she made sure the students recog-
nized these words as they appeared in reading assignments and also
pointed out other words related to them. A few minutes spent playing with roots such as *chrono-* (time) and *chromo-* (color) or suffixes such as *-phile* (love) and *-phobe* (fear) can help students
build vocabulary from what they already know as well as introduce
them to new words.

A day or two devoted to dictionary usage early in the term is
always extremely beneficial. All students assume they know what a
dictionary's purpose is, but few of them know how to use it effectively or how to interpret its abbreviations and symbols. They also
assume any dictionary is just as good as every other. Section 38
in the *Handbook* gives an excellent introduction to dictionary usage,
and many publishers will provide classroom study guides for their
dictionaries upon request. Since the dictionary should be as important to the composition student as his or her pen and paper, an
early and careful examination of the "word book" is essential.

The dictionary is also a good starting point for an exploration
of exactness in word usage. You have undoubtedly graded papers
that were obviously written with large, and misapplied, doses from
a thesaurus. A discussion of connotation and denotation can go a

long way toward curing rampant "thesaurusitus." Many students are not aware that synonyms do not mean exactly the same thing. A little dictionary work with synonyms will often help to develop an awareness of the precise meanings of words. Approximate homonyms, as they are discussed in section 40b, represent an area which causes a great deal of confusion in written communications. You can get a few laughs as well as make an important point by explaining the face-reddening errors that can result if one "eludes" to something rather than "alludes" to it, or if one speaks of a couple having "martial" difficulties rather than "marital" difficulties. Closely associated to exactness is directness, and the exercises in section 41 will help students who believe quantities of words and involved expressions are emblematic of intellectuality.

SECTION 38

THE DICTIONARY

Few will deny the importance of the dictionary to the student. Too often, however, the dictionary ends up somewhat like Mark Twain's weather--everybody talks about it, but nobody does anything about it. The result is that many students get all the way through high school and college with no more than a nodding acquaintance with a work which could benefit them greatly--if they knew how to use it.

What to do about it, then, is the problem. Section 38 of the *Handbook* provides an extensive basis for instructors who would like to establish a dictionary unit; other instructors who desire to spend a limited amount of time on the dictionary will want to use only some of its exercises.

An activity you may find profitable is to require your students to compare several desk dictionaries on such aspects as pronunciation, etymology, clarity of meaning, synonymies, nature of grammatical treatment, and labels. Such a comparison can be made of the sample word *howl* discussed in section 38 of the text or, if reproductive facilities are available, you can distribute copies of pages from various dictionaries which deal as much as possible with the same range of words.

Still another way is to prepare handout sheets providing complete dictionary entries of four or five words from the best desk dictionaries. Comparing the handout sheets, students can be asked to indicate differences among the entries from different dictionaries and in what respects any of the dictionaries surpass the others. These comments, in turn, can be made the basis for a composition with such titles as "The Best Standard Desk Dictionary," "The Characteristics of a Good Desk Dictionary," "What I Like About the *New World Dictionary*," "A Comparison of Etymological Development in the Most Widely Used Standard Desk Dictionaries," and many other similar subjects. Writing a composition about dictionaries based upon a study of dictionaries has the advantage of imposing a unified overall approach to the subject--one which requires the student to perform some basic research prior to the time he or she writes. As such, then, it satisfies a dual function. It gives the student something to write about, and it provides a meaningful approach whereby the student can learn a great deal about the dictionary.

For another beneficial exercise, you might have students examine the *Oxford English Dictionary*. Using a word list you have prepared, they can write paragraphs explaining how the meanings of several words have changed over the years, citing a word's earliest appearance in the language and subsequent definitions with references to examples in the *O.E.D.* Since the *O.E.D.* is now also available as *The Compact Edition of the Oxford English Dictionary*, you might want to obtain the two-volume set and take it to class for some on-the-spot work.

Having become familiar with dictionaries, students sometimes get "hooked" on derivations, etymologies, and definitions. More than one instructor has walked into the classroom to find students engrossed in reading dictionary entries. One class's dictionary work led to a round of marathon dorm Scrabble games and renewed enthusiasm for crossword puzzles.

Section 38 provides several other good exercises requiring students to explore thoroughly what their own dictionaries have to offer. These fact-finding activities involve such things as preferred spelling [38(1)], hyphenization [38(2)], foreign and naturalized terms [38(3)]. Exercises 38(4) and 38(5) focus on word pronunciation, and exercise 38(6-8) discusses etymology. Other exercises in the unit emphasize word meanings, grammatical information, usage labels, and the parts of the dictionary.

Exercise 38(1)

In this and subsequent dictionary exercises, some variation may be expected since the major desk dictionaries show minor variations. Where answers provided are based on a single dictionary, that dictionary is indicated in parenthesis after the exercise number.

OR esthetic	demon	licorice
OR catalog	enclose *OR* inclose	*OR* modelled
OR ketchup	favor	Shakespeare
criticize	*OR* judgment	*OR* theater

Exercise 38(2)

bookshop	jazzmen	supermarket
castoff	passkey	up-to-date
easygoing	self-government	well marked
horse race	showdown	worldwide

Exercise 38(3)

(Reference: *Webster's New World Dictionary,*
Second College Edition)

Note that dictionaries vary widely in this matter. Some consider it too subjective a matter to be prescribed.

bon voyage	*dramatis personnae*	résumé
coup d'etat	matinee (or matinée)	*sine qua non*
creche	*nouveau riche*	*Weltschmertz*
debutante		

Exercise 38(4)

(Reference: *Webster's New World Dictionary,*
Second College Edition)

ə dult', ad'ult   eks'kwi zit, ik. skwiz'it

ā'lē əs, āl'yəs   fôr'mə də b'l

ser' ə brəl, sa rē' brəl   jen' yoo wən

des' pik ə b'l, di spik' ə b'l   grē' sē, grē' zē

                                    im' pə tənt

                                    mis' chi vəs

                                    ri sʉrch', rē' sʉrch

                                    rōot, rout

Exercise 38(5)

1. French; Medieval Latin *assassinus;* Arabic hashshāshĩn,
    hashish eaters < *hashish,* hemp

2. Middle English *Bedlem, Bethlem* < the London hospital of St.
    Mary of Bethlehem

3. Blend of *drag* and drabble

4. Middle English *egg, egge* < Old Norse *egg* < Anglo-Saxon *aeg*
    (probable Indo-European base *owjom-, *ojom,* laid by a bird)

5. Middle English and Old French *familier;* Latin *familiaris,* of
    a household, domestic < *familia*

6. French; fedora (1882), play by Sardou

7. Medieval Latin *incisivus* < Latin *incisus,* past participle of
    incidere, to cut into < *in-,* into + *caedere,* to cut.

8. French; *lampoon* < *lampons,* let us drink--refrain in a drinking
    song < *lamper,* to drink

9. Middle English *neighbour,* nyebour; Anglo-Saxon *neaghbur* <
    neah, nigh (basic sense, "turned toward, looking toward") +
    gebur, freeholder, peasant, farmer

10. Middle English *organizacion* < Medieval Latin *organizatio*

11. Middle English *prest, preost;* Anglo-Sazon *preast* < Late Latin
    presbyter, an elder; Greek *presbyteros,* elder, comparative of
    presbys, old, an old man. (cf. Sanskrit *purugava,* a guide,
    leader, originally of a herd of oxen)

12. After John Montagu, 4th Earl of *Sandwich* (1718-1792), said to
    have eaten these in order not to leave the gaming table for
    meals

13. Middle English *schirte, schurte;* Anglo-Saxon *scyrte* < *skurti < base of *scort,* shert; akin to German *schurze,* apron, doublet of English *skirt;* basic sense "short garment"

14. Middle English; Old Norse *skyrt,* shirt, *kirtle,* exactly cognate with Anglo-Saxon *scyrte* (see *shirt* above)

15. Gaelic *sluggh-ghairn* < *sluagh,* a host + *gairm,* a call

16. < earlier *quelch* (fusion of *quell* and *crush*) with *s-* intensifier

Exercise 38(6)

1. André Marie Ampère, French physicist and mathematician.

2. Captain Boycott, land agent ostracized by his neighbors during the Land League agitation in Ireland in 1880.

3. Nicolas Chauvin, soldier of Napoleon I, notorious for his bellicose attachment to the lost imperial cause.

4. Johns Duns Scotus, called the "Subtle Doctor" (died c. 1308) whose followers, called *Dunsmen, Duncemen* and Renaissance humanism; the word came to be applied to any opponent of education, and then to a stupid person.

5. Alexander Gorden (1730-1791), American botanist.

6. John L. MacAdam (1756-1836), Scottish engineer who invented the process.

7. Vidkun Quisling (1887-1945), Norwegian politician who betrayed his country and became its puppet ruler.

8. General H. Shrapnel (1761-1842), of the British Army, who invented it.

9. Ulster, Ireland, where originally made and worn.

10. James Watt (1736-1819), Scottish inventor.

Exercise 38(7)

1. almanac - Arabic

2. cherub - Hebrew

3. cockatoo - Malayan

4. dory - American Indian (Central America)

5. goulash - Hungarian

6. huckster - Middle English or Middle Dutch

7. jute - East Indian, Sanskrit

8. kerosene - Greek

9. moccasin - American Indian (Algonquin)

10. mukluk - Eskimo

11. piano - Italian

12. squadron - Italian

13. trek - South African Dutch

14. tulip - Turkish

15. typhoon - Chinese

Exercise 38(8)

Dictionaries vary widely in method of listing. (The following is based on the *American College Dictionary*)

call - 43	land - 17	run - 104
get - 20	light - 64	set - 67
go - 43	out - 55	turn - 93
high - 32		

Exercise 38(9)

(*Webster's New Collegiate*)

1. bounty - 1. liberality in giving: generosity; 2. something that is given generously; 3. yield esp. of a crop; 4. a reward, premium, or subsidy esp. when offered or given by a government: as (a) a grant to encourage an industry (b) a payment to encourage the destruction of noxious animals

2. complexion - 1. the combination of the hot, cold, moist, and dry qualities held in medieval physiology to determine the quality of a body; 2. (a) an individual complex of ways of thinking or feeling; (b) a complex of attitudes and inclinations; 3. the hue or appearance of the skin and esp. of the face; 4. general appearance or impression

3. engine - 1. *obs.* (a) ingenuity; (b) evil contrivance; wile; 2. *archaic:* something used to effect a purpose; agent; 3. (a) a mechanical tool: as (1) an instrument or machine of war (2) *obs.* a torture implement (b) machinery (c) any of various mechanical appliances--compare fire engine; 4. a machine for converting any of various forms of energy into mechanical force and motion; 5. a railroad locomotive

4. fond - 1. foolish, silly (--pride); 2. (a) prizing highly; desirous (--of praise) (b) strongly attracted or predisposed (of music); 3. (a) foolishly tender; indulgent (a--mother) (b) loving, affectionate (a--wife); 4. doted on: dear (his --est hopes)

5. generous - 1. *archaic:* highborn; 2. (a) characterized by a noble or forbearing spirit; magnanimous, kindly; (b) liberal in giving; openhanded; (c) marked by abundance or ample proportions; copious (d) full-flavored (--wine)

6. gossip - 1. *dial. Brit:* godparent; (b) companion, crony; (c) a person who habitually reveals personal or sensational facts; 2. (a) rumor or report of an intimate nature; (b) a chatty talk

7. humor - 1. (a) a normal functioning fluid or semifluid of the body; (b) a secretion that is an excitant of activity; 2. (a) *in medieval physiology;* a fluid or juice of an animal or plant: specif: one of the four fluids entering into the constitution of the body and determining by their relative proportions a person's health and temperament; (b) habit, temperament; (c) temporary state of mind; (d) a sudden, unpredictable, or unreasoning inclination: whim; 3. (a) that quality which appeals to a sense of the ludicrous or absurdly incongruous; (b) the mental faculty of discovering, expressing, or appreciating the ludicrous or absurdly incongruous; (c) something that is or is designed to be comical or amusing

8. intern - 1. adj. *archaic* (a) internal; 2. to confine or impound esp. during a war; 3. intern or interne: an advanced student or graduate esp. in medicine gaining supervised practical experience (as in a hospital)

9. knave - 1. *archaic* (a) a boy servant; (b) a male servant; (c) a man of humble birth or position; 2. a tricky deceitful fellow; rogue, rascal; 3. Jack: a playing card carrying the figure of a soldier or servant and ranking usually below the queen

10. lozenge - 1. a figure with four equal sides and two acute and two obtuse angles; diamond; 2. something shaped like a lozenge; specifically: a small, often medicated candy

11. machine - 1. (a) *archaic:* a constructed thing whether material or immaterial; (b) conveyance, vehicle; specifically: automobile; (c) *archaic:* a military engine; (d) any of various apparatus formerly used to produce stage effects; (e-1.) an assemblage of parts that transmit forces, motion, and energy one to ano her in a predetermined manner; (2) an instrument (as a ever) designed to transmit or modify the application of power, force or motion; 2. (a) a living organism or one of its functional systems; (b) a person or organization that acts for a common end together with the agencies they use; (s) a highly organized political group under the leadership of a boss or small clique; 3. a literary device or contrivance introduced for dramatic effect

12. manufacture - 1. something made from raw materials; 2. (a) the process of making wares by hand or by machinery especially when carried on systematically with division of labor; (b) a productive industry using mechanical power and machinery; 3. the act or process of producing something

114

13. sincere - 1. (a) free of dissimulation: not hypocritical: honest (a--friend) (--interest); (b) free from adulteration: pure (--doctrine) (--wine); 2. marked by genuineness: real, true (a--work of art)

14. starve - 1. (a) to perish from lack of food; (b) to suffer extreme hunger; 2. *archaic* (a) to die of cold; (b) to suffer greatly from cold; 3. to suffer or perish from deprivation

15. virtue - 1. (a) conformity to a standard of right: morality; (b) a particular moral excellence; 2. *cap:* an angel of the fifth highest rank; 3. a beneficial quality or power of a thing; 4. manly strength or courage: valor; 5. a commendable quality or trait: merit; 6. a capacity to act: potency; 7. chastity, especially in a woman.

Exercise 38(10)

Note that the student will not find *all* of these items listed under synonymies in any one dictionary. In addition, students must follow cross references to locate synonymies for certain items.

AMBITIOUS, ASPIRING, ENTERPRISING describe one who wishes to rise above his present position or condition. The AMBITIOUS man wishes to attain worldly success, and puts forth effort to this end: *Ambitious for social position.* The ENTERPRISING man, interested especially in wealth, is characterized by energy and daring in undertaking projects. The ASPIRING man wishes to rise (mentally or spiritually) to a higher level or plane, or to attain some end that he feels to be above his ordinary expectations.

LIKELY, APT, LIABLE are not alike in indicating probability; though APT is used colloquially, and LIABLE mistakenly, in this sense. LIKELY is the only one of these words which means "probable" or to be expected: *it is likely to rain today.* Hence APT comes to be associated with LIKELY and to be used formally as a substitute for it: *he is apt at drawing, he is apt to do well at drawing.* LIABLE should not be used to mean "probable." When used with an infinitive, it may remind one of LIKELY: *he is liable to be arrested.* But the true meaning, susceptibility to something unpleasant, or exposure to risk, becomes evident when it is used with a prepositional phrase: *he is liable to arrest, liable to error.*

MUTUAL may be used of an interchange of feeling between two persons (John and Joe are *mutual* enemies) or may imply a sharing jointly with others (the *mutual* efforts of a group); COMMON implies a being shared by others or by all the members of a group (our *common* interests).

DEFACE, DISFIGURE mean to mar the appearance of. DEFACE implies superficial injuries (as by scratching, scribbling, or the removal of detail); DISFIGURE suggests deeper and more permanent injuries.

DIPLOMATIC, POLITIC, TACTFUL imply ability to avoid offending others or hurting their feelings, especially in situations where this is important. DIPLOMATIC suggests a smoothness and skill in handling others, usually in such a way as to attain one's own ends and yet avoid any unpleasantness or opposition: *by diplomatic conduct he avoided antagonizing anyone.* POLITIC emphasizes expediency or prudence in looking out for one's own interests, thus knowing how to treat people of different types and on different occasions: *a truth which is not politic to insist on.* TACTFUL suggests a nice touch in the handling of delicate matters or situations and, unlike the other two, often suggests a sincere desire not to hurt the feelings of others: *a tactful wife.*

FAMOUS is the general word: *a famous lighthouse.* CELEBRATED originally referred to something commemorated, but now usually refers to someone or something widely known for conspicuous merit, services, etc.: *a celebrated writer.* EMINENT implies high standing among one's contemporaries, especially in his own profession or craft: *an eminent physician.*

HUGE, ENORMOUS, IMMENSE imply great magnitude. HUGE, when used of concrete objects, usually adds the idea of massiveness, bulkiness, or even shapelessness: *a huge mass of rock, a huge collection of antiques.* ENORMOUS, literally out of the norm, applies to what exceeds in extent, magnitude, or degree, a norm or standard: *an enormous iceberg, enormous curiosity.* IMMENSE, literally not measureable, is particularly applicable to what is exceedingly great, without reference to a standard: *immense buildings.* All are used figuratively: *a huge success, enormous curiosity, immense joy.*

EQUANIMITY implies an inherent evenness of temper or disposition that is not easily disturbed; COMPOSURE implies the disciplining of one's emotions in a trying situation or habitual self-possession in the face of excitement.

RESTIVE describes one who is balky, contrary, fidgety, stubbornly resisting control. A RESTLESS person is uneasy, unable to stop moving or to relax, always seeking activity or change.

RAVENOUS, VORACIOUS suggest a greediness for food and usually intense hunger. RAVENOUS implies extreme hunger, or a famished condition: *ravenous wild beasts.* VORACIOUS implies the eating of a great deal of food, or the disposition to eat a great deal without reference to the degree of hunger (*a voracious small boy incessantly eating*) or figuratively (*a voracious reader*).

Exercise 38(11)

broadcast or broadcasted, broadcasting

focused or focussed, focusing or focussing

dived or dove, diving

got, getting

lent, lending

shrank or shrunk, shrinking

set, setting

taught, teaching

waked or woke, waking

alumni

bears or bear

courts-martial

crises

daisies

fish or fishes (referring to
different species)

indexes or indices

mesdames

strata or stratums

Exercise 38(13)

worse, worst

worse, worst

littler or less or lesser,
littlest or least

lengthier, lengthiest

more, most

oftener, oftenest

redder, reddest

more shyly, most shyly

better, best

Exercise 38(14)

1. Corny - Standard in the sense of "of or producing corn."
    Slang in the sense of "countrified, old-fashioned, trite,
    sentimental." (WNW) Colloquial when applied to jazz "written
    or played with self-conscious emotionalism, lacking sophisti-
    cation or spontaneity or enthusiasm" (ACD)

2. Cool - Standard in reference to temperature. Colloquial in
    the sense of "without exaggeration: as he lost a cool million
    on the deal." Slang in the sense of "very good, pleasing,
    etc.; excellent"

3. Flap - Standard in the sense of a hanging part, the movement
    of such a part, or the noise produced by such a part. *Collo-
    quial* to toss, fold, shut, etc., smartly, roughly, or noisily
    (ACD). *Slang* an occasion of excited activity; emergency;
    crisis

4. Foul-up - [Colloq.], to make a mess of; make disordered or
    confused; entangle or bungle (WNW). To throw into disorder or
    confusion; to blunder (SCD)

5. Goof - Slang

6. Hipster - Slang

7. Jerk - Standard when used as a verb. Slang in the sense of
    "a person regarded as stupid, dull, eccentric, etc."

8. Kibitzer - Colloquial

9. Moll - Slang in the sense of a gangster's mistress or a pros-
    titute

10. Snollygoster - Standard (listed only in W7)

11. Wise-up - Slang

12. Yak - Standard in reference to the animal. Slang in sense of "laugh" or "joke" (listed only in W7)

Exercise 38(15)

1. billabong - Australia

2. chuckwagon - Western United States

3. coulee - Western North America

4. hoecake - Southern United States

5. laager - South Africa

6. petrol - Britain

7. potlatch - Northern Pacific coast (American Indian)

8. pukka - India

9. snarpie - New England

Exercise 38(16)

1. embarrass

2. en'və.lōp (or än'va.lōp)

3. French précis < Latin *praecisus*, past participle of *praecidere* to cut off < *prae*-before + *caedere* to cut

4. rain, rein

5. diffuse, prolix, wordy, redundant

6. re-dun-dant

7. right, accurate, exact, precise

8. synonym, synonymous, synonymy; valve, vector, verb, verse, version, versus, vice-, vocative, voice, volt, voltage, volume, vow; museum, music, musical, musician; Roman Catholic Church

9. Look at the end; Art is long, life is short; From out of the depths; Shame be to him who thinks evil of it

10. 25, 525

11. Bill of exchange

12. 693 miles

13. Charlotte

14. Hebrew

15. since, rinse, wince, quince, prince, evince, convince

VOCABULARY

A natural and often simultaneous result of dictionary work is vocabulary building. The overview preface for sections 38-44 in this manual describes some techniques for teaching vocabulary in your composition class. If you use a reader or collection of stories in addition to the *Handbook* for your course, vocabulary lists can be generated from assigned readings. Many texts provide definitions at the bottoms of pages or word lists at the ends of stories and essays.

Another profitable area of study is prefixes and suffixes such as those listed in section 39 of the *Handbook*. Exercises 39 (1-6) involve working with these prefixes and suffixes. Exercise 39(8) can give students good training in utilizing synonymies to distinguish between words of similar meaning.

Exercise 39(1)

inaccuracy	nonconformity	immutable
unadorned	indistinctive	irrational
disagreeable	inexplicable	unworkable

Exercise 39(2)

decentralize	disintegrate	displease
undo	demagnetize	disqualify
disinherit	dissuade	unravel

(But note that "dissuade" is defined as "persuade not to do" and that "ravel" can mean both "entangle" and "disentangle.")

Exercise 39(3)

advancement	denial	promotion
calculation	helplessness	rebellion
disappearance	judgment	statesmanship

Exercise 39(4)

advisor(or)	communicator	profiter
boaster	disturber	sailor
commander	preacher	saver

beautify	idolize	moralize
blacken	liquify	pacify
captivate	modernize	victimize

Exercise 39(6)

humorous	restful (less)	thwarted
ironic (ical)	speedy	waspish
mulish	talkative	whimsical

Exercise 39(7)

Only the more common meanings are listed here. Specialized meanings are omitted. The reference is *Webster's New World Dictionary,* Second College Edition

1. compatible - capable of living together harmoniously or getting along well together; in agreement; congruous

2. demagogue - orig.) a leader of the common people; a person who tries to stir up the people by appeals to emotion, prejudice, etc. in order to win them over quickly and so gain power

3. intimidate - to make timid; make afraid; overawe; to force or deter with threats or violence; cow

4. disparage - to lower in esteem; discredit; to speak slightingly of; show disrespect for; belittle

5. ostentatious - characterized by or given to ostentation; showy; pretentious

6. altruistic - of or motivated by altruism. altruism - unselfish concern for the welfare of others; selflessness

7. taciturn - almost always silent; not liking to talk; uncommunicative

8. malign - *v.t.* to speak evil of; defame; slander; traduce

9. unscrupulous - not scrupulous; not restrained by ideas of right and wrong; unprincipled

10. officious - offering unnecessary and unwanted advice or services; meddlesome, esp. in a highhanded or overbearing way

11. facetious - joking or trying to be jocular; esp. at an inappropriate time

12. incentive - stimulating one to take action, work harder, etc.; encouraging; motivating. *noun* - something that stimulates one to take action, work harder, etc.; stimulus, encouragement

13. ambiguous - having two or more possible meanings; not clear; indefinite; uncertain; vague

14. pragmatic - having to do with the affairs of a state or community; concerned with actual practice, everyday affairs, etc., not with theory or speculation; practical

15. estrangement - *verb, estrange* - to remove, as from usual surroundings or associates; keep apart or away; to turn (a person) from an affectionate or friendly attitude to an indifferent, unfriendly, or hostile one; alienate the affections of

16. promiscuous - consisting of different elements mixed together or mingled without sorting or discrimination; characterized by a lack of discrimination; specif. - engaging in sexual intercourse indiscriminately or with many persons; without plan or purpose; casual

17. euphoria - a feeling of vigor, well-being, or high spirits, specif. - *psychol.* one that is exaggerated and without an obvious cause

18. corpulent - fat; fleshy; stout; obese

19. transcend - to go beyond the limits of; overstep; exceed (a story that transcends belief); to be superior to; surpass; excel

20. pompous - full of pomp; stately; magnificent; characterized by exaggerated stateliness; pretentious, as in speech or manner; self-important

21. finite - having measurable or definable limits; not infinite

Exercise 39(8)

Distinctions in meanings are based on synonyms in *Webster's New World Dictionary*, Second College Edition. In instances where synonyms do not cover all of the given words, meanings of words not given therein are those reflected by definitions accompanying the main entry words.

1. *quality*, the broadest in scope of these terms, refers to a characteristic (physical or nonphysical, individual or typical), that constitutes the basic nature of a thing or is one of its distinguishing features (the *quality* of mercy); *property* applies to any quality that belongs to a thing by reason of the essential nature of the thing (elasticity is a *property* of rubber); *character* is the scientific or formal term for a distinctive or peculiar quality of an individual or of a class, species, etc. (a *hereditary* character); an attribute is a quality assigned to a thing, especially one

that may reasonably be deduced as appropriate to it (omnipotence is an *attribute* of God)

2. *neglect* implies a failure to carry out some expected or required action, either through carelessness or by intention (I *neglected* to wind the clock); *omit,* in this connection, implies a neglecting through oversight, absorption, etc. (she should not *omit* to visit the Louvre); *disregard* implies inattention or neglect, usually intentional (she always *disregards* his wishes); *ignore* suggests a deliberate disregarding, sometimes through stubborn refusal to face the facts (but you *ignore* the necessity for action); *overlook* suggests a failure to see or to take action, either inadvertently or indulgently (I'll *overlook* your errors this time)

3. *costly* refers to something that costs much and usually implies richness, magnificence, rareness, etc. (*costly* gems): it is often applied to that which it would cost much in money or effort to correct or replace (a *costly* error); *expensive* implies a price in excess of an article's worth or of the purchaser's ability to pay (an *expensive* hat); *valuable,* in this connection, implies such great value as to bring a high price (a *valuable* collection); *precious* is of great price or value; *priceless* is of inestimable value, beyond price

4. *calm,* basically applied to the weather, suggests a total absence of agitation or disturbance (a *calm* sea, mind, answer); *tranquil* implies a more intrinsic or permanent peace and quiet than *calm* (they lead a *tranquil* life); *serene* suggests an exalted tranquility (he died with a *serene* smile on his lips); *placid* implies an undisturbed or unruffled calm and is sometimes used in jocular disparagement to suggest dull equanimity (she's as *placid* as a cow); *peaceful* suggests a lack of turbulence or disorder (a *peaceful* gathering)

5. *eager* implies great enthusiasm, zeal, or sometimes impatience, in the desire for or pursuit of something (*eager* to begin work); *avid* suggests an intense, sometimes greedy, desire to enjoy or possess something (*avid* for power); *keen* implies deep interest and a spirited readiness to achieve something (the team was *keen* on winning); *anxious,* in this connection, suggests an eagerness that is accompanied with some uneasiness over the outcome (*anxious* to do his best)

6. *puzzle* implies such a baffling quality or such intricacy, as of a problem, situation, etc., that one has great difficulty in understanding or solving it; *perplex,* in addition, implies uncertainty or even worry as to what to think, say, or do; *bewilder* implies such utter confusion that the mind is staggered beyond the ability to think clearly; *dumbfound* specifically implies as its effect a nonplussed or confounded state in which one is momentarily struck speechless

7. *fashion* is the prevailing custom in dress, manners, speech, etc., of a particular place or time, esp. as established by the dominant section of society or the leaders in the fields of art, literature, etc.; *style* often a close synonym for fashion, in discriminating use suggests a distinctive fashion, esp. the way of dressing, living, etc., that distinguishes persons with money and taste; *vogue* stresses the general

acceptance or great popularity of a certain fashion; *fad* stresses the impulsive enthusiasm with which a fashion is taken up for a *short* time; *rage* and *craze* both stress an intense, sometimes irrational enthusiasm for a passing fashion

8. *adjust* describes the bringing of things into proper relation through the use of skill or judgment (to *adjust* brakes; to *adjust* differences); *conform* means to make the same or similar (to *conform* one's values to another's); *reconcile* is to settle (a quarrel, etc.), or compose (a difference, etc.)

9. *correct* connotes little more than absence of error (a *correct* answer) or adherence to conventionality (*correct* behavior); *accurate* implies a positive exercise of care to obtain conformity with fact or truth (an *accurate* account of the events); *exact* stresses perfect conformity to fact, truth, or some standard (the *exact* time, an *exact* quotation); *precise* suggests fastidious attitude (*precise* in all his habits)

10. *hinder* implies a holding back of something about to begin and connotes a thwarting of progress; *obstruct* implies a retarding of passage or progress by placing obstacles in the way; *block* implies the complete, but not necessarily permanent, obstruction of a passage or progress; *impede* suggests a slowing up of movement or progress by interfering with normal action; *bar* implies an obstructing as if by means of a barrier; *dam* means (1) to keep back by means of a dam; hence, (2) to keep back or confine (usually with *in* or *up*)

11. *ghastly* suggests the horror aroused by the sight or suggestion of death; *grim* implies hideously repellent aspects; *grisly* suggests an appearance that causes one to shudder with horror; *gruesome* suggests the fear and loathing aroused by something horrible and sinister; *macabre* implies concern with gruesome aspects of death

12. *plan* refers to any detailed method formulated beforehand, for doing or making something; *design* stresses the final outcome of a plan and implies the use of skill or craft, sometimes in an unfavorable sense, in executing or arranging this; *scheme*, a less definite term than the preceding, often connotes either an impractical, visionary plan or an underhand intrigue; *plot* is used of a secret, usually evil, project or scheme the details of which have been carefully worked out.

13. *copy* implies as nearly exact imitation or reproduction as is possible; *mimic* suggests close imitation, often in fun or ridicule; *mock* implies imitation with the intent to deride or affront; *ape* implies close imitation either in mimicry or in servile emulation

14. *maudlin* is that which is tearfully or weakly sentimental in a foolish way (an intoxicated, *maudlin* guest); *mushy* is a colloquial expression meaning the same as *maudlin*; *sentimental* suggests emotion of a kind that is felt in a nostalgic or tender mood (*sentimental* music) or emotion that is exaggerated, affected, foolish, etc. (a trashy, *sentimental* novel)

15. *malice* implies a deep-seated animosity that delights in causing others to suffer or in seeing them suffer; *spite* suggests a mean desire to hurt, annoy, or frustrate others, usually as displayed in petty, vindictive acts; *grudge* implies ill will inspired by resentment over a grievance.

EXACTNESS

Since section 40 concerns itself with the exact meanings of
words, various exercises are provided to assist student understanding in such matters as confusion of words with similar sounds or
spelling but with different meanings, improprieties, changes in
meaning from one suffixal form of a word to another, elegant variation, and idiomatic use of words and phrases. The list of idiomatic prepositions used after verbs and adjectives that is given in
section 40f may prove particularly helpful to students.

Exercise 40a(1)

1. A *garish* person is vulgarly showy. Substitute *exciting, spark-
   ling, brilliant, stirring*, etc.

2. *Obstinacy* is unreasonable inflexibility. Substitute *fearless-
   ness, firmness, courage, boldness, doggedness*, etc.

3. *Displeasure* is a state of annoyance or irritation, but
   the context of the sentence suggests an affront to the
   ambassador's sense of dignity. Substitute *indignation*.

4. A *pretext* is a fictitious reason or motive advanced to conceal
   a real one. Substitute *reason, justification*, etc.

5. A *pedantic* person makes needless display of his learning and
   insists on the importance of trifling points of scholarship.
   Substitute *learned*.

Exercise 40a(2)

1. *ignorant* - implies a lack of knowledge, either generally (an
   ignorant man) or on some particular subject (*ignorant* of the
   reason for their quarrel); *illiterate* implies a failure to
   conform to some standard of knowledge, esp. an inability to
   read or write; *unlettered* often implies unfamiliarity with
   fine literature (although a graduate engineer, he is relatively *unlettered)*; *uneducated* and *untutored* imply a lack of formal systematic education, as of that acquired in schools (his
   brilliant, though *uneducated* mind).

2. *detached* - implies an impartiality or aloofness resulting from
   a lack of emotional involvement in a situation (he viewed the
   struggle with *detached* interest); *disinterested* strictly implies a commendable impartiality resulting from a lack of self-
   ish motive or desire for personal gain (a *disinterested*
   journalist), but it is now often used colloquially to mean not
   interested, or indifferent; *indifferent* implies either apathy
   or neutrality, esp. with reference to choice (to remain *indifferent* in a dispute); *unconcerned* implies a lack of concern,
   solicitude, or anxiety, as because of callousness, ingenuous-

ness, etc. (to remain *unconcerned* in a time of danger).

3. *excuse* - implies a passing over of a fault, omission, or failure without censure or due punishment in view of extenuating circumstances; *condone* suggests an accepting without protest or censure some reprehensible act or condition; *pardon* implies the freeing from the penalty due for admitted or proved offense; *forgive* implies the giving up not only of any claim to requital or retribution but also of any resentment or desire for revenge.

4. *rebellion* - implies open, organized, and often armed resistance to authority; *revolution* applies to a successful rebellion resulting in a change usually in government; *insurrection* implies an armed uprising that quickly fails or succeeds; *mutiny* applies to group insubordination or insurrection esp. against maritime or naval authority.

5. *fierce* - applies to men and animals that inspire terror because of their wild and menacing aspect or fury in attack; *ferocious* implies extreme fierceness and unrestrained violence and brutality; *barbarous* implies a ferocity or mercilessness regarded as unworthy of civilized men; *savage* implies the absence of inhibitions restraining civilized men filled with rage, lust, or other violent passion; *cruel* implies indifference to suffering and even positive pleasure in inflicting it; *inhuman* implies a lack of those characteristics considered normal to human beings.

Exercise 40b

(American College)

1. *adapt* - to make suitable to requirements; *adept* - one who has attained proficiency; *adopt* - to choose for or take to oneself

2. *alley* - a narrow, back street; *ally* - to unite by marriage, treaty, league, or confederacy

3. *allude* - to make an allusion; *elude* - to avoid or escape by dexterity or artifice

4. *anecdote* - a short narrative of a particular incident or occurrence of an interesting nature; *antidote* - a medicine or other remedy for counteracting injurious effects

5. *anesthetic* - a substance such as ether, chloroform, cocaine, etc., that produces anesthesia; *antiseptic* - pertaining to or affecting antisepsis

6. *angel* - one of a class of spiritual beings, attendants of God; *angle* - the space within two lines or three planes diverging from a common line

7. *arraign* - to call or bring before a court to answer to a charge or accusation; *arrange* - to place in proper, desired, or convenient order

127

8. *bloc* - a coalition of factions or parties for a particular measure or purpose; *block* - a solid mass of wood, stone, etc., usually with one or more plane or approximately plane faces

9. *borne* - pp. of *bear* in all meanings except in the sense "brought forth" where *born* is now used; *born* - brought forth by birth

10. *Calvary* - Golgotha, the place where Jesus was crucified; *cavalry* - that part of a military force composed of troops that serve on horseback

11. *cannon* - a mounted gun for firing heavy projectiles; *canon* - an ecclesiastical rule or law enacted by a council or other competent authority

12. *canvas* - a closely woven, heavy cloth of hemp, flax or cotton, used for tents, sails, etc.; *canvass* - to examine carefully

13. *carton* - a cardboard box; *cartoon* - a sketch or drawing as in a newspaper or periodical, symbolizing or caricaturing some subject or person of current interest in an exaggerated way

14. *chord* - a string of a musical instrument; a combination of three or more tones in harmonic relation; *cord* - a string or small rope composed of several strands twisted or woven together

15. *climatic* - pertaining to or forming a climax; *climactic* - pertaining to weather conditions of a region.

16. *confidently* - having strong belief or full assurance; *confidentially* - spoken or written in confidence

17. *costume* - the style of dress, including ornaments and the way of wearing the hair, esp. that belonging to a nation, class, or period; *custom* - a habitual practice

18. *elicit* - to draw or bring out or forth; *illicit* - not permitted or authorized

19. *epic* - denoting or pertaining to poetic composition in which a series of heroic achievements or events, usually of a hero, is dealt with at length as a continuous narrative in elevated style; *epoch* - a particular period of time as marked by distinctive character, events, etc.

20. *flaunt* - to parade or display oneself conspicuously or boldly; *flout* - to mock, scoff at, treat with disdain or contempt

21. *genteel* - belonging or suited to polite society; *gentile* - of or pertaining to any people not Jewish

22. *historic* - well-known or important in history; *historical* - relating to or concerned with history or historical events

23. *human* - of, pertaining to, or characteristic of man; *humane* - characterized by tenderness and compassion for the suffering or distressed

24. *ingenious* - (of things, actions, etc.) showing cleverness of inventive faculty; *ingenuous* - free from reserve, restraint, or dissimulation

25. *marital* - of or pertaining to marriage; *martial* - inclined or disposed to war

26. *morality* - conformity to the rules of right conduct; *mortality* - the condition of being mortal or subject to death

27. *prescribe* - to lay down in writing or otherwise, as a rule or a course to be followed; *proscribe* - to denounce or condemn (a thing) as dangerous

28. *receipt* - a written acknowledgment of having received money, goods, etc., specified; *recipe* - any formula, esp. one for preparing a dish in cookery

29. *statue* - a representation of a person or an animal carved in stone or wood, molded in a plastic material, or cast in bronze or the like; *statute* - an enactment made by a legislature and expressed in a formal document

30. *waive* - to forbear to insist on; *wave* - a disturbance of the surface of a liquid body, as the sea or a lake, in the form of a ridge or swell

Exercise 40c

1. *savagery*, not *savagism*

2. *nonpolitical*, not *unpolitical*

3. *unpredictable* is acceptable

4. *liberal*, not *liberalistic*

5. *has stoplights*, not *is stoplighted*

6. *roof* is acceptable

7. *bulldoze* is acceptable

8. *toweled* is acceptable

9. *vacation*, not *holiday*

10. *drive our jeep*, not *to jeep*

Exercise 40d

1. An *arguable* point is open to dispute or question; an *argued* point has been or is being disputed or questioned.

2. A *practical* solution is one that seems to have met the demands of actual living or use; a *practicable* solution is one that seems feasible but has not been actually tested in use.

3. A *hated* person is intensely disliked; a *hateful* person excites or deserves hate.

4. A *liberal* foreign minister is one who is an advocate of liberalism; a *liberated* foreign minister is one who has been set at liberty.

5. A *single* effect is only one effect; a *singular* effect is an extraordinary or an unusual effect.

6. An *intelligible* writer is capable of being understood; an *intelligent* writer is one with good understanding or mental capacity.

7. A *godly* man is pious; a *godlike* man is like God or a god.

8. An *informed* teacher possesses knowledge or information; an *informative* teacher communicates information.

9. A *peaceful* nation is free from strife; a *peaceable* nation is inclined to avoid strife.

10. A *workable* arrangement is capable of being worked; a *working* arrangement is one that works.

11. An *amicable* teacher is friendly, peaceable; an *amiable* teacher is pleasing in disposition.

12. A *yellow* piece of paper is of a bright color like that of ripe lemons; a *yellowed* piece of paper has changed (with age) to a sallow color.

Exercise 40e(2)

The paragraph uses a number of hackneyed terms as it refers to Marty Jerome: *diminutive, pint-sized, little fellow, mighty mite, the tiny Jerome,* and *little man.* In referring to his activities it describes them in such terms as *scampered, bulled, hit the ground, 85 long and magnificent yards, rabbit-run, bullet-like plunges, like a streak of light,* and *bulled his way over.* In referring to game action such terms are employed as *final frame, marker, pay-dirt, last frame, tallies,* and *home base.*

Exercise 40f(1)

1. to, with
2. of, from
3. to, with
4. for, into
5. with, to
6. with, to
7. to(with), with
8. from, to(for)
9. to(of), to
10. into, to

SECTION 41

DIRECTNESS

One of the most difficult points to get across to students is that the clearest and best writing is the simplest and most direct. At some point in their schooling they have been led to believe that "sounding educated" means writing pompous, wordy, convoluted prose. Or they may have developed a "padded" style as a defense against having "nothing to say."

Prying students away from such propensities is like taking candy from a baby; in either instance, to pursue the comparison to its ultimate, unless matters are corrected, the results can become rather messy. To assist in this area, section 41 of the *Handbook* provides discussions and exercises on deadwood, circumlocutions, awkward repetition, and simple, direct expression.

You might mention to your students that complicated, high-flown language rarely impresses anyone. In fact, people in the business, technical, and professional world become annoyed when pretentious wordiness taxes their time and energy. Exercise 41a-f is good for testing student understanding of direct expression.

Exercise 41a

1. He is an expert in labor relations.

2. The fastest automobile requires the best gasoline.

3. Most Congressmen spend most of their working days attending committee meetings.

4. Dr. Mackenzie has more ability and experience than Dr. Smith.

5. People can be taught to plan good, inexpensive, and nutritional menus.

6. The steady, two weeks' rain is washing away the seeds I planted.

7. Mr. Armstrong, my history teacher, had a dynamic classroom manner.

8. I am not going because I have an examination and no money.

9. Love and understanding are two of the most important things young children need.

10. After several hours of shopping, I gave my mother a check so she could buy her own gift.

11. After he finished his navy service, he decided to re-enroll in school.

1. Jim jogged every morning at 7 a.m. because he believed in exercise.

2. This book explains the fundamentals of English.

3. Barbara Linger's black limousine has been parked a number of times in front of Blickel's market.

4. It was the student consensus that grades be abandoned.

5. Teachers should illustrate grammatical rules they are trying to teach.

6. Joyce is a very difficult writer to read.

7. He is an industrial engineering student studying time-and-motion.

8. I believe government should not intervene in private business.

9. A reckless driver is no better than a murderer.

10. Last night we had to circle the block before finding a parking space.

Exercise 41a-f

1. The United States cannot expect to spread peace to other countries until we teach our own people to respect each other.

2. He is capable of working long hours each day.

3. The integration of public schools is a major step toward equality.

4. During his whole college career, Peter planned to work his way around the world.

5. Only in the past couple of years have black Americans begun to make it clear that they wish to develop their own racial identity.

6. Nixon chose Agnew as a running-mate for Vice-President because he wanted a Southern candidate as a nominee.

7. The first settlers in the West explored as they prospected for gold.

8. The actress performed very badly, but the play continued to its end.

9. He was the handsomest man I had ever seen.

10. Pollution in our waterways has troubled scientists for one and a half decades.

SECTION 42

APPROPRIATENESS

Although instructors may vary somewhat in the level of writing they will accept from their students, few will accept anything less than an informal level. The differences, of course, among formal, informal, and nonstandard levels are not always readily apparent to the student. For this reason, section 42 explores aspects of usage such as slang, regional and nonstandard English, trite expressions, jargon, stilted diction, and mixed and incongruous metaphors. Sometimes, as you will want to point out to your students, what is suitable for one audience will not be suitable for another. Exercise 42a-f gives students practice in deciding whether or not the diction employed in some sample writing is suitable for certain types of audiences. The "Diction" Review Exercise is a good test over exactness, directness, and appropriateness in writing.

Exercise 42c(1)

wily Indians; to strike while the iron was hot; the break of dawn; The hardy pioneers; in unison; veritable hail of bullets; the pesky redskins keeled over and bit the dust; The rugged frontiersmen; to give a good account of themselves; broad daylight; broke through the ramparts; their backs against the wall; slaughtered mercilessly; When the dust had risen from the battlefield; when the smoke had cleared away; carnage was frightful; Every single; gone to meet his maker.

Exercise 42c(2)

The American Way ... feasible route ... to tread; educational personnel; education institutions of learning; humble origins; child of adversity; born in a log cabin; beyond a shadow of a doubt; reached the summits; fair country of ours; There is too much of a tendency to view ... with alarm; great institution; But on the other hand; people who live in glass houses; the type most inclined to cast aspersions; wet blankets; the ones by whom criticisms are made; Now I'm just ... should be run; Abe Lincoln, if he were alive; newfangled techniques; making a shambles of; at the bottom of; our American heritage; the American Way; notorious radicals; wreaked havoc with our boys and girls.

Exercise 42f

1. He encountered a disastrous eddy as he swam through the sea of life.

2. Jim brought his big guns to the debate and shot down his opponent.

134

3. The scent of the flowers on the table greeted us with an aromatic welcome.

4. The young teacher is rapidly gaining stature in the eyes of the student.

5. We're skating on thin ice and if it breaks we'll enjoy a cold water bath.

6. The Senate wanted to plug the loopholes in the tax bill but it couldn't because too many important people were interested in keeping them open.

7. He worked as busily as a beaver, but one day he became so ill that he decided to do a little less dam building in the future.

8. My constantly misplacing my glasses makes me blind, although I know my apartment as a bat knows his cave.

9. Although she was head over heels in love with him, she still managed a level head about the matter.

10. He had his back to the wall; then he had his inspiration and he was able to move forward.

"Words" Review Exercise (Sections 40 through 42)

1. He was trying to keep abreast of company developments; but because he kept getting behind, his reputation ebbed.

2. A college student has to study a lot if he is going to be a successful student.

3. C. B. Brown must have worked very hard to complete six Gothic novels in less than four years.

4. Many beginning Bilingual Education instructors are weak in instructional methodology.

5. Indications are that one Joshua Fiddings wrote the novel.

6. The campus police theorized that the burglars entered through the cafe.

7. My little sister's pretty face becomes very red when my brother beats her unmercifully in ping-pong.

8. Mr. Smith was the bane of his wife's existence because he frequently forgot her shopping instructions.

9. We shall do all we can to make you comfortable.

10. Professor Caitlin was poor financially, but he was so well regarded that more students in the college remembered him than any other teacher.

11. Coaches are paid for teams that win games.

12. The house was square and painted blue, and he decided it was a good buy for the money.

13. I thought I was doing the best thing when I enlisted in the army.

14. I was filled with anger when my expensive stereo equipment was destroyed by the vandals. (*rage, precious,* and *ruined* can be substituted for *anger, expensive,* and *destroyed.*)

15. By reading *Yachting,* I am able to keep informed about sailing activities.

SECTION 43

GLOSSARY OF USAGE

The Glossary of Usage is a directory of levels of usage for various words and expressions. It is probably most helpful as a reference chapter, and you can advise students to familiarize themselves with its alphabetical listing. When they are in doubt about the acceptability of an expression, the Glossary may provide the answer.

SPELLING

Spelling is an area of considerable challenge to many college students. While it is true that spelling is an elementary school subject, it is one elementary school subject that has not been too well mastered. In the college classroom, then, the instructor is placed in a dilemma. Composition class seems a rather late stage for the learning of proper spelling; on the other hand, if students cannot spell well, you, as the instructor, can scarcely afford the luxury of ignoring the situation. At the same time, a composition course is not a spelling course; therefore, you will have to decide how you can do the most about deficiencies in the limited time that can reasonably be devoted to the matter.

Section 44 may benefit some students. Many of the time-tested rules which aid correct spelling are given; lists of commonly mispronounced and frequently misspelled words are also included. You may want to require your students to learn these words. While testing from the lists will not solve all their spelling problems, students should also be encouraged to keep a list of the words they repeatedly misspell and concentrate on the most frequent offenders.

Many students repeatedly misspell words that are pronounced the same or about the same (e.g. *their, they're, there; too, two, to; here* and *hear; its* and *it's*). In these cases you can stress that what is involved is not simply misspelling but rather a misunderstanding of the words' function. In other words, students may be helped to avoid misspelling the variant forms of *their, they're* and *there* if they understand that *their* is the possessive of *they* and hence is an adjective; *there,* on the other hand, is usually an adverb indicating place; and by comparison, *they're* is a contraction for *they are.* Similarly, *too* is an adverb denoting intensification of the word it modifies; *to* is either a preposition or part of an infinitive; *two* of course indicates a number. By the same token, *its* and *it's* often give a great deal of trouble which can be avoided once the student understands that *it* is one of the few words whose possessive form is indicated without the use of an apostrophe and that *it's* is never possessive, but a contraction of *it is.*

Exercise 44e(1)

Rule notations refer to paragraphs wherein the rule is discussed in text.

argument - exception to rule 2b

beggar - rule 4

buried - rule 3

conceivable - rule 2a

eightieth - rule 3

association - rule 2a

hoping - rule 2

drooping - rule 4

changeable - exception to rule 2a

changing - rule 2

awful - exception to rule 2b

precedence - rule 2

shining - rule 2

business - rule 3

deferred - rule 4

peaceable - exception to rule 2a

Exercise 44e(2)

Rule notations refer to paragraphs wherein the rule is discussed in text.

1. frames, rule 5
2. roses, rule 5
3. branches, rule 6
4. basses, rule 6
5. echoes, rule 6
6. strata, rule 9
7. Charleses, rule 6
8. noes, rule 6
9. dashes, rule 6
10. mazes, rule 5
11. tables, rule 5
12. cameos, rule 5
13. flies, rule 7
14. boxes, rule 6
15. churches, rule 6
16. ladies, rule 7
17. masses, rule 6
18. potatoes, rule 6
19. plays, rule 8
20. pains, rule 5

THE LIBRARY AND THE RESEARCH PAPER

Like the dictionary, the library can be of tremendous assistance to students, but all too frequently they spend four years on a college campus without discovering much more in their library than the card catalog and the *Reader's Guide*. The smallest library contains a wealth of resources that would surprise many students. One way to insure that your class learns to use at least some of these resources is to give a library familiarization assignment.

You can lead an instructional tour of the campus facility yourself. On the other hand, many college libraries provide self-guided library tour pamphlets including a library quiz for students to complete as they proceed from location to location in the library. If your library does not have such a pamphlet, you and the reference librarian might discuss developing one. Similarly, in many libraries staff members will give orientation sessions and tours on request. Frequently, the staff will tailor the orientation to include specific areas of study as well as general references. Libraries are usually very eager to publicize their facilities and teach students how to get the most benefit from them.

Section 43 contains a list of some of the most important reference books including, first of all, guides to reference books, general encyclopedias, dictionaries, word books, year books, atlases and gazeteers, general biographies, and books of quotations. Also listed are reference books relating to mythology and folklore, modern literature, history, music and painting, philosophy and religion, science and technology, and social sciences. Indexes to periodicals, bulletins, and pamphlets are also listed: the widely used *Reader's Guide to Periodical Literature* and *Index to the Social Science and Humanities* and many special indexes relating to specific disciplines.

Section 46 explains a systematic approach to writing a research paper, beginning with a discussion of how to choose and limit a topic, and ending with the presentation and discussion of a specimen research paper. A number of sample bibliographical and footnote entries are given--enough to satisfy most questions concerning the majority of situations involving types of entries with which students will be confronted.

The specimen research paper is very thoroughly discussed; the comments on a paragraph-by-paragraph basis concerning the composition of the paper and the manner in which footnote entries have been made will probably anticipate and answer a number of your students' questions.

SECTION 45

THE LIBRARY

Section 45 discusses such important aspects of the library as catalogs, catalog cards, and library holdings in general. Three very practical exercises are provided which will require students to investigate the library and use some of its resources.

Exercise 45(1) requires the student to go to the library and to indicate on a diagram the locations of twenty-five of the most widely used reference books and indexes. You may want to prepare a diagram of your library's reference room on a handout sheet, asking students to insert the numbers of the various works on this sheet. This saves the student time and makes it possible to assign additional work in the library in lieu of time spent in drawing the diagram.

Exercise 45(2) requires the student to answer questions by consulting reference books in the library. It is a good idea to have students prepare their answers in complete sentences and to italicize the work from which they obtained the answer. This requirement achieves training in writing good sentences and in italicizing book and periodical titles.

Exercise 45(3) requires students to examine reference works in some detail and to summarize properly the information such works contain. A start in proper documentation can be made with this exercise if you ask students to quote material taken from these works in the preparation of the exercise.

Exercise 45(2)

1. *The Jewish Encyclopedia*, 8, pp. 493-495.

2. Tlingit tribe. *Encyclopedia of Religion and Ethics*, XI, 443.

3. For two partners: 1 rocker; 1 dipper; 2 buckets (to carry the dirt in); 2 shovels; 1 pick; 1 pan. *Encyclopedia Americana*, XI, 524b.

4. In 12th-century England, *gossip* meant "a godparent." (*Oxford English Dictionary*).

5. Five. *Education Index*, XI, 898. (Twelve articles are listed for period June 1957-June 1959.)

6. *International Index*, XIV and XV.

7. *Agricultural Index* and *Industrial Arts Index*.

8. *Art Index*, X and XI ("Glass painting and staining, French").

9. Washing machine. *Dictionary of American Biography*, V, 410.

10. *Dictionary of National Biography*, 16, p. 788.

11. $5.19 (Publishers Library Binding), Pantheon.

12. 1021. *Statistical Abstract of The United States*, 1971, p. 568.

SECTION 46

THE RESEARCH PAPER

Instructor attitudes toward the research paper in composition courses vary widely at present. There appears to be more and more of a trend toward the writing of a short documented paper of 1000-1500 words in lieu of the longer research paper that has often been favored in the past. The reasoning behind this change in point of view takes into consideration many factors, not the least of which is that some English departments now offer a separate research report writing course.

Another factor is the regrettable tendency on the part of many students to copy excerpts from many different sources into one synthesized whole and to present the final effort as an original one. Unfortunately, even though the ends of research may have been somewhat served by such activity, the more important aspect of dealing with the research paper in an honest, professional manner has not. Of course, writing a shorter paper will not in itself result in an absence of plagiarism, inadvertent or otherwise, but the mere fact that the writing assignment is relatively short, and hence will involve fewer research sources, tends to put the emphasis on documentation and proper summarization rather than on a frenzied gathering of material from diverse sources.

As a further end to proper documentation and summarization, some instructors prefer to use a good case book. A case book involves the disadvantage of lack of original research; however, many contend that first things come first and, hence, learning how to properly extract and report from other sources is the skill that is most important in the initial stages of the student's research writing career. In other words, learning how to handle properly the research material must occur before any accurate, meaningful account of research activities can take place.

Other instructors feel that learning to use the library is an important part of the purpose behind research paper writing, and they prefer to avoid case books. Control and safeguards against plagiarism can still be maintained if you require your students to submit portions of their work at various stages of the research paper project. For example, you can ask for a topic proposal, a working bibliography, a thesis statement and working outline, and a rough draft of the paper before the final draft is prepared. You can also have students submit all their note cards with the final draft as well as run a check on note-taking form a week or two after note-taking has begun. Not only does this procedure cut down substantially on plagiarism, it provides useful feedback to the students while they still have time to make changes in their papers before the final grade is assigned.

Several of your students may wish to deviate from the approach to research paper writing presented in the *Handbook*. This can be especially true of note-taking, since students frequently prefer to take their notes on notebook paper instead of cards. The methods described in the text are time-honored and field-tested. Card note-taking is recommended because it is more efficient and enables the writer to arrange all of his or her notes into an easily handled sequence for the actual writing task. While you may want to allow some flexibility on various aspects of the paper writing process, you should point out to your students that the procedures delineated by the *Handbook* present a *method:* one fundamental reason for a research paper assignment is to teach students a systematic, efficient method that can be applied to any research/ writing situation. It is not uncommon for students who finish a research paper according to the prescribed procedure to comment that they wish they had been taught "the method" much earlier in their academic careers--because *it works.*

Section 46 discusses the choosing and limiting of a research paper topic, and Exercise 46(1) presents a list of questions. As students obtain the answers to these questions, they should discover an idea for a good research paper subject. Of course, if you have assigned a novel or other reading from which all students' papers will be derived, you may wish to compose your own list of questions for topic development. The technique of asking questions about a prospective subject area is good in that it helps provide the students with some initial positive direction. If a particular question intrigues them, they may become quite interested in getting the answer to that question. This is the very essence of constructive research--to learn something about a subject that one wishes to know about.

A number of good specimen bibliography cards and exercises relating to the handling of bibliographical entries are supplied in the text. Exercises 46 (3) and 46(4) provide good practical working experience for the student in preparing bibliographical cards and short working bibliographies.

At the time you are dealing with note-taking, you will want to assign work involving summarization, and several of the exercises in section 47 can help. Effective summarization and quotation is perhaps, more than anything else, the most important and the most difficult phase of the research paper. Much of the plagiarism that occurs in research papers is inadvertent and results not from deliberate dishonesty on the part of the student but from a lack of ability to present in his or her own words what it is that someone else has said. Students also need to be reminded that whenever they use the ideas of others, even if not presented as direct quotations, they need to document these ideas with a footnote. In any case, developing the ability to summarize accurately and skillfully is a monumentally difficult task, and positive results in this respect will not be easy to come by. Any degree of success, consequently, will usually be achieved only through sustained and repetitive endeavor.

Several aspects of note-taking can be emphasized which will assist in the proper utilization of note cards. First of all, the students can be made to understand that note cards can be of at least three types:

(1) *the note card which involves the copying of material from another source.* You will need to emphasize that when-

ever material is taken directly from another source, it must be included in quotation marks. Insist that students put the quotation marks on all note cards which record verbatim source material. This way they will recognize that the words are those of another when they are using the note card to write their papers, and they will give proper credit when incorporating the material into the paper draft.

(2) *the note card which contains the student's summarization of what another source says.* You will want to stress that students should summarize, if possible, without looking directly at the source material. In short, if students can be trained to write their summarization by closing the reference source before preparing their account, what will result will be their own words and not those of the original author.

(3) *the note card which contains only words and phrases from another source.* This is often a good type of note card to emphasize, since it requires students to elaborate in their own words upon ideas or comments of others, or upon factual material.

The requirement that all three types of notes be used should result in a research paper which strikes a happy balance between quotations and summarizations--one which will avoid plagiarism.

The question of how to handle footnote cards can be a vexing one. In particular, the reconciliation of footnote entries to the note cards can be a very tedious and time-consuming task for you as you grade research papers. One effective and timesaving procedure is the following: require students to insert blank sheets of paper between the successive typed pages of their papers and then to staple the footnote cards which pertain to footnotes on a particular page to the reverse side of the blank sheet which precedes that page. If students are further required to key the footnote card according to the superscript, a very systematic basis for your review is provided. After all, you are primarily interested in how the footnote cards were used in developing the text of the paper, not the number of cards as such. Using this method, you can, as you evaluate the paper, quickly determine the effectiveness of the way the footnote material has been used by comparing what is on the footnote cards on the left page with what is in the text of the term paper page on the right.

A number of specimen footnotes are included in the text of section 46. These samples should provide adequate assistance in the majority of footnoting situations the student is likely to face. Since not all disciplines require or even accept the *MLA Style Sheet* documentation form used for the sample references in the *Handbook,* you should mention that when writing research papers for special fields, students should use the documentation forms prevalent in those fields. Again, emphasize to them that while the details of documentation forms may differ, the logical systemization behind them all is the same. The University of Chicago Press *Manual of Style* enjoys wide academic acceptance.

Section 46(8) discusses briefly some ways to introduce quoted material. You will want to elaborate on the possible methods for integrating quotations, since students tend to "chop and drop" quotations without any transition from their words to those of their source. This produces paragraphs of a distinctly distracting nature--paragraphs with "hiccups." Students also tend to assume that the meaning or relevance of a quotation is self-evident, so you may want to point out that they should provide analysis and commentary where appropriate.

It may be quite profitable to spend considerable time in class going over the specimen paper in section 46. The text authors have provided many penetrating comments on the specimen paper concerning why the research writer has prepared the paper in that way that she has. You will probably want to discuss several of these points to insure that your students thoroughly understand the methods that have been employed in writing the paper.

SECTIONS 47-48

WRITING SUMMARIES AND EXAMINATIONS

Section 47 is a short section of the *Prentice-Hall Handbook for Writers;* nevertheless, it is a very important one. As has already been mentioned in the manual remarks in section 46, students' ability to put into their own words what others have said is all-important in the proper development of a research paper. Unfortunately, a great number of students cannot do this and will be unable to do it without a great deal of practice.

Section 47 provides a good discussion of how to approach a summarization task, stressing first that the student should attempt to determine the author's purpose and point of view. In effect, the student is isolating the controlling or main idea, practicing the ability to get quickly to the core of the material. This ability is the key to writing good summaries.

Exercises 47(1)-47(4) require students to construct sentence precis of various paragraphs. All provide good training in identifying main ideas and presenting them in condensed, precise prose. If you want to assign additional summarization exercises besides 47(1) in the text, you can ask students to prepare summaries of paragraphs or essays from a reader or assigned magazine.

A variation in the writing of summaries can be achieved by asking students to write two different summary versions of a paragraph, one which involves a quotation or two from the paragraph, and another which does not. Still another summarization technique useful to students pertains to quoting one author who is quoting another (this may involve a quotation within a quotation). You might choose a paragraph or two for duplication which reports the remarks of one person on the work or remarks of another. Students would then have to write their own summaries of the discussion. Literary criticism or political commentaries are good sources for this assignment.

Exercise 47(1)

The purpose of good teaching is to train youngsters not only to learn but to study on their own. Training students to think is more important than requiring them to memorize things.

Exercise 47(2)

The purpose of good teaching is to train students to work things out for themselves rather than to memorize.

Exercise 47(3)

Students who participate in dietary training benefit because they learn about people from other sections, they mature, and they become more independent and self-sufficient.

Exercise 47(4)

Nothing, neither torrents of rain nor endless portraits of Stalin, can dampen the enthusiasm of Russians for their pageants and popular feasts; and they insist that their foreign guests enjoy the pretty girls, the flowers, the floats, the dancing and singing and marching as much as, and as late as, they do.

Examinations are so much a part of academic life that we tend to forget they do require a deliberate approach. Many students have not learned good study habits in high school, and for them writing examinations is almost a hit-or-miss proposition, no matter how well they have prepared the subject matter. For students returning to school after a period of absence for work or family raising, exams are a real trial because study habits of several years past have been largely forgotten. Some students blindly memorize every bit of data they can, hoping the exam will cover something they have committed to memory. Others flounder aimlessly among the trivia in their textbooks, unable to sift what is important from what is minor. And many students cannot determine from their lecture notes those points an instructor has emphasized, i.e. will probably ask on a test. You will be doing most of your students a great service if you at least point out to them the existence of section 48.

Section 48 discusses such things as reading exam questions carefully, something students frequently fail to do, much to their chagrin later. It also emphasizes the use of a thesis statement for controlling the contents of an essay-test answer, as well as marshaling supporting facts and detail to add depth and development to test responses.

Eventually most students learn to "psych out" probable test questions as they study for an exam, but any additional advice you can give will be much appreciated by your class.

SECTION 49

BUSINESS LETTERS

Section 49 is provided not so much for composition students as for the general audience of writers who use the *Prentice-Hall Handbook* as a reference work. On the other hand, since many composition instructors are now emphasizing "real world" writing applications in their classes, section 49 may play a role at some point in a composition course. Particularly if you are teaching a remedial class, you may want to adapt some assignments to fit writing situations students are likely to face at home or at work. The guiding principles of a business letter are the same as those of a composition: purpose, point, support and development, unity, coherence, and clarity.

Section 49 details the six parts of a business letter, types of business letters, and letter formats. A number of sample letters are provided to show students how the finished product should look. Assigning the writing of a letter to handle some special situation such as a complaint, an inquiry, or a job application is one way to generate directed writing early in the semester when your primary goal is to collect diagnostic material for evaluating a class's strengths and weaknesses.

SECTION 50

A GLOSSARY OF GRAMMATICAL TERMS

Section 50 is probably not one that you will want to assign for class discussion since it is, in effect, a capsule explanation of various terms which are treated more fully in other parts of the text. It is nonetheless a section which can be very valuable for quick reference purposes, and you should familiarize yourself with it so you can direct students to the Glossary if they are having trouble understanding some particular aspect of grammar. Sometimes reading an explanation in slightly different phraseology will provide the glimmer of comprehension that unfolds a previously troublesome term or concept.

This section can also give a quick overall review of the grammar section of the *Handbook*. As such it can help students determine for themselves the extent to which they understand the various grammatical terms and perhaps motivate them to review aspects which they still do not understand too well.